World War II Wargames Rules

BOLT ACTION

Armies of the
SOVIET UNION

Written by: Andy Chambers

Edited by: Rick Priestley and Alessio Cavatore

Cover artwork: Peter Dennis

Interior Artwork: Peter Dennis
and Ron Volstad

Photography: Warwick Kinrade, Mark Owen, Rick Priestley
and Paul Sawyer

Artefacts: John Stallard Collection.

Miniatures painted by: Simon Bargery, Neil Burt,
Andrés Amián Fernández, Stephan Huber, Alan Mander
and Gary Martin.

Thanks to: Simon Bargery, Andrew Chesney, Wojtek Flis,
Paul Hicks, David Holmes, Dave Lawrence, Bernard Lewis,
Paul Sawyer and John Stallard

D1602183

OSPREY
PUBLISHING

WARLORD
GAMES

ospreypublishing.com
warlordgames.com

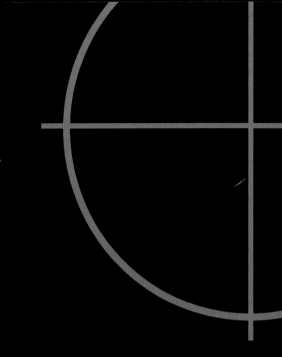

First published in Great Britain in 2013 by Osprey Publishing Ltd.

© 2013 Osprey Publishing Ltd. and Warlord Games

Osprey Publishing
Midland House, West Way, Botley, Oxford, OX2 0PH, UK
43-01 21st Street, Suite 220B, Long Island City, NY 11101, USA
E-mail: info@ospreypublishing.com

Osprey Publishing is part of the Osprey Group

Warlord Games
T04/T10 Technology Wing, The Howitt Building, Lenton Business Centre,
Lenton Boulevard, Nottingham, NG7 2BD
E-mail: info@warlordgames.com

A CIP catalogue record for this book is available from the British Library

Print ISBN: 978 1 78096 090 6

Page layout by: PDQ Media, Bungay, UK
Typeset in Univers and Nidex

Originated by PDQ Digital Media, Bungay, UK
Printed in China through Worldprint Ltd.

13 14 15 16 17   10 9 8 7 6 5 4 3 2 1

Osprey Publishing is supporting the Woodland Trust, the UK's leading
woodland conservation charity, by funding the dedication of trees.

www.ospreypublishing.com

For more information on Bolt Action and other products, please visit www.warlordgames.com

Paj Lowinger
(562) 441-3666

CONTENTS

WHAT IS THIS BOOK?

The Soviet 8th Army attempts to break out at the Dunaburg bridgehead, 28 June 1941, by Peter Dennis © Osprey Publishing Ltd.
Taken from Campaign 148: Operation Barbarossa 1941 (2).

This book is a supplement for the Bolt Action World War II tabletop wargame. It contains all the background, rules and Army List information needed to field a Soviet Army in the Bolt Action game. Inside you'll find details of organisation and equipment covering the Soviet Union's Red Army forces from the beginning of what came to be called the Great Patriotic War (22 June 1941, the opening day of operation Barbarossa) to the end of the war in Europe (7 May 1945, the surrender of Germany).

As you will see, the main Army List includes all the necessary gaming details for all the troop types, vehicles and equipment fielded by the Soviets in World War II. Alongside this main list you will find 18 specific Theatre Selectors. These indicate which kinds of troops, weapons and vehicles are available during different phases of the war and in different theatres on the Eastern Front. While the Soviet Union had the largest army in the world at the beginning of the German-led invasion, it proved no match for the elite Panzer divisions that had brought Europe to its knees. Four years of bitter fighting, unthinkable hardship and incalculable determination enabled the Soviet Union to eventually emerge victorious over Nazi Germany.

To avoid a lot of pointless repetition, the main Army List includes all the rules needed for each kind of unit as well as all the options potentially available to it. The Theatre Selectors narrow this information down as appropriate to that specific campaign or phase of the war. The Theatre Selectors indicate the predominant kinds of troops and equipment available during a campaign or at a certain time, but exceptions are perfectly allowable so long as both players agree.

A Maxim medium machine gun covers the Soviet advance

THE RED ARMY OF WORLD WAR II

"The constant urge to get to grips with the enemy with the aim of destroying him, must lie at the basis of the training and activity of every commander and soldier of the Red Army. Without special orders to this effect the enemy must be attacked boldly and with dash wherever he is discovered."
– Provisional Field Service Regulations of the Workers' and Peasants' Red Army (People's Commissariat for Defence 1937)

THE OCTOBER REVOLUTION AND THE CIVIL WAR

Tsarist Russia became the object of mass discontent among its subjects during the final years of World War I. Severe economic decline, repeated defeats on the battlefield, unemployment, bankruptcy and runaway debt combined to motivate a series of general strikes and popular uprisings against Tsar Nicholas II in what came to be called the February Revolution. A provisional government was formed under Prince Lvov (later Alexander Kerensky) in an attempt to mediate the demands of the workers and peasants with the military and aristocracy.

Under pressure from the Western Allies (France, the United Kingdom, the United States of America and Japan), the provisional government declared its intention to continue the war with Germany. This, and attempted repression of the peasants, led to the overthrow of the provisional government by the Marxist–Leninist Bolshevik party in October 1917. This precipitated a four year long civil war between the predominantly Bolshevik 'Reds' and the so-called 'White Army' – a loose federation of monarchists, anti-communists and nationalists actively supported by the Western Allies (who also landed their own troops in parts of Russia and occupied them for two years).

THE RED ARMY

The assorted pro-communist combat forces loyal to the Bolsheviks organised themselves into the 'Workers and Peasants Red Army' (*Raboce-Krestjanskaja Krasnaja Armija*  – the RKKA). They fought against the White Army (as well as the anti-communist *and* anti-white 'Black' and 'Green' armies) in a wide-ranging campaign that forged the reputations of many individuals who later served as part of the Communist Central Committee. A young Josef Stalin, for example, led the Red Army forces that held Tsartisyn on the Volga river against the Whites, which led to the city later being renamed Stalingrad. From 1919 to 1921 the Red Army was also involved in the Polish–Soviet war but, after initial success, suffered a major setback that (temporarily) put paid to Soviet ambitions in Poland.

The Red Army began life as a voluntary organisation, but became a conscript force by decree of the People's Council of Commissars in May 1918. All males between the ages of 18 and 40 were eligible for military service. Typically, two years of full-time service were required before becoming a reservist, while career officers formed a permanent cadre. Numerous regional military commissariats (abbreviated to *Voyenkomat*) handled the formation and training of divisions.

Strategic direction of the enormous Red Army was provided by the *Stavka*, a military council of the highest ranked Red Army commanders (Stavka is derived from an old Russian word for 'tent'). Nominally, the Stavka was presided over by the defence minister of the central committee but during the Great Patriotic War it was entirely subject to the will of Stalin

Red Army infantry support an SU-122M assault gun

and, increasingly as the war progressed, the Soviet Union's finest military mind – Marshal Zhukov.

The Red Army was highly progressive in its thinking in the 1930s. It embraced the role of aircraft and tanks for achieving breakthroughs in much the same way the resurgent German army was doing with its concept of *Blitzkrieg*. It also pioneered the development of paratroops, gliders, self-propelled and rocket artillery. Until 1933, the Red Army and the German Heer had surprisingly close ties with German officers training secretly in the Soviet Union to avoid the restrictions placed on them by the hated Treaty of Versailles. The rise of the Nazi party in Germany ended any kind of co-operation. Hitler was a vehement anti-Bolshevist and dreamt of 'liberating' the lands of the east to create new fiefdoms for his thousand-year Reich.

The Red Army participated in several major conflicts that allowed it to test some of its theories and equipment. During the Spanish Civil War the Soviet Union gave help to the Republicans and tested their new generation of tanks and aircraft against German-built (and often German-crewed)

opponents. In the Far East the Red Army fought successfully against the Japanese and Chinese armies to keep control of Manchuria and Mongolia. Xinjiang was also invaded and a pro-Soviet government installed there. The growing quality of the Red Army, however, was about to be sharply diminished.

THE PURGES

Starting in 1937, Josef Stalin orchestrated a series of 'purges' against Communist party membership, government officials, Red Army officers, the peasantry, ethnic groups and just about everybody else to consolidate his power under the guise of crushing fabricated 'counter-revolutionary' plots. It was a time of widespread surveillance, suspicion, mass arrests, imprisonment, torture, show trials, deportations and executions. Between 1937 and 1942, millions were exiled to remote and inhospitable regions of the Soviet Union, while hundreds of thousands more (some historians say millions) were executed by the NKVD.

REBORN IN BATTLE, THE EVOLUTION OF THE RED ARMY

'My XXIX Corps has 8,706 men left. Facing it are 69,000 Russians. My XVII corps has 9,284 men: facing it are 49,500 Russians, My IV Corps is relatively best off – it has 13,143 men, faced by 18,000 Russians. Altogether 31,133 Germans against 136,500 Russians. The relative strength in armour is similar: Tolbukhin yesterday had 165 tanks in operation: we had seven tanks and thirty-eight assault guns.' – General Hollidt to Hitler, 27 August 1943.

In 1941 and the early part of 1942, The Red Army often relied on mass tactics of World War I vintage. Attacks were made on a broad front without dedicated support from tanks and aircraft. The Germans were amazed by the sight of great masses of infantry advancing against machine guns shoulder-to-shoulder with bayonets fixed, singing and shouting 'Urrai!' as they charged to their doom. Constant attacks were viewed as essential to the role of the Red Army in tying down and wearing out the enemy, but mindlessly repeated frontal assaults in areas where they had previously failed simply added to the carnage.

Events in the first year of war forced the Red Army to revise its tactics. The defence of Stalingrad proved that the Germans could be beaten only by fixing their attention to a strategic objective and then striking back with overwhelming force when the opportunity presented itself. Zhukov and other survivors of the purges revived the concept of 'deep operations' – using massed armour to strike through fissures opened in the enemies' defence by intensive combined arms attacks on narrow fronts. The Soviets also became masters of the art of *Maskirovka*, military deception used to conceal the movement and massing of armies, or to misdirect enemy attacks onto dummy positions.

As the Red Army turned the tide and moved west its commanders learned how best to exploit their advantages, in particular their overwhelming numbers. The occasional local successes enjoyed by the Germans counted for little against the strategic backdrop of the whole of the Eastern Front as the Soviets simply bypassed them and drove ever deeper into the Reich.

The purges hit the leadership of the armed forces very hard. At the head of the Red Army, three out of its five marshals were removed, 13 out of 15 army commanders, eight out of nine admirals, 50 out of 57 corps commanders, 154 out of 186 divisional commanders, all 16 of the army commissars and 25 out of 28 army corps commissars. Not all of these were killed

– many were expelled from the Communist party and sentenced to decades of hard labour in the gulags for their 'crimes' instead.

The immediate loss of experienced officers capable of handling higher level formations in the Red Army was critical. Even beyond that, however, the purges left behind a climate of

The Red Army prepares to pound German positions with their 120mm heavy mortar.

The defence of Brest Fortress by troops of the Soviet 6th Rifle Division, by Peter Dennis © Osprey Publishing Ltd. Taken from Campaign 186: Operation Barbarossa 1941 (3).

fear that suppressed innovation and independence in the survivors. For the most part the Red Army reverted to old-fashioned World War I thinking, nervously obeying its orders to the letter without regard to actual circumstances. While such drone-like obedience was desirable for the State it made for poor soldiers, as would be proved in the Russo–Finnish War.

THE RUSSO-FINNISH WAR

In 1939 the Soviet Union signed a non-aggression pact with Germany that gave Stalin a free hand to annex the Baltic States (Latvia, Lithuania and Estonia), eastern Poland and Finland. Finland had declared its independence from collapsing Imperial Russia in December 1917, and had gained recognition from the Bolshevik government shortly afterwards. Several peace agreements signed over the intervening years were ignored when the Red Army struck in December 1939.

The assembled Soviet forces outnumbered the tiny Finnish army by three to one in men, thirty to one in tanks and a hundred to one in aircraft. The ponderous Red Army, however, performed abysmally against the highly motivated Finnish

forces in the sub-zero temperatures of what became known as the Winter War. Entire divisions of Soviet troops were cut off and ambushed by Finnish battalions in the thick forests of Karelia. Scores of Soviet tanks were burned, artillery and masses of equipment were captured, and the Red Army was utterly humiliated.

Though the Red Army (heavily reinforced) eventually managed to force a peace agreement on the Finns in early 1940, international opinion was firmly behind 'plucky Finland'. What had been thought of as a foregone conclusion in fact gave a stark demonstration that, despite their enormous numbers, the armed forces of the Soviet Union were a paper tiger.

The Red Army began a vast reorganization, and new equipment was rushed into service in light of experiences in Finland, but it was already too late. Hitler and the leaders of the Wehrmacht had taken note of the Red Army's lack of ability. Once Western Europe was beneath their heel they turned their rapacious gaze to the east. While the Battle of Britain still raged in the skies over southern England, plans were already being drawn up for the conquest and exploitation of the Soviet Union.

MOTHER RUSSIA

'In spite of the distances we were advancing there was no feeling, as there had been in France, of entry into a defeated nation. Instead there was resistance, always resistance, no matter how hopeless. A single gun, a group of men with rifles... once a chap ran out of a cottage by the roadside with a grenade in each hand...' – Anonymous captain of the 18th Panzer Division, Summer 1941.

The war in the east was completely unlike the fighting the Germans experienced in Western Europe. For one thing, continental Russia encompassed distances that were vast to Western European eyes, with Moscow lying some seven hundred and fifty kilometres from the Polish border. A great hinterland of untamed forests and swamps separates the major towns and cities of the north, with the great Pripyat marshes occupying much of southern Belorussia. In 1941 roads were few and often little more than unpaved dirt tracks that the Germans called *Rollbahns* ('runways'). In bad weather these roads quickly turned into muddy quagmires that trapped wheeled and even tracked vehicles in their glutinous embrace.

In autumn and spring Russia, Belorussia and the Ukraine are gripped by the *raputista* (literally 'quagmire season') when heavy rains or thawing snows saturate the ground. At these times the roads became completely impassable for a month or more, a fact that some historians believe robbed the Germans of their momentum at a critical moment. Even without the *raputitsa*, however, the Germans were already suffering mechanical problems with their overworked vehicles and supply shortages due to the huge distances everything had to travel.

As a result, the rail networks proved vital for moving large amounts of material on the Eastern Front. Control of towns and cities that were at the nexus of different railway lines became a key feature of campaigns. When the Germans first invaded, though, they were frustrated in this regard too as the Soviet railway system used a different gauge to that of Germany and Poland. The large numbers of Soviet partisans operating behind the front lines attacked the German-held railways remorselessly throughout the Great Patriotic War. With partisans, infiltrating cavalry units and large numbers of 'surrounded' Red Army soldiers a constant threat to rear echelon units, it often seemed to the Germans as if the entirety of the vast land was against them.

The most deadly aspect of the Eastern Front was its harsh winters, something for which the Germans were entirely unprepared in 1941. By the end of the year, the forces struggling towards Moscow had suffered as many casualties from frostbite as they had from enemy action. Sentries froze to death at their posts. Weapons jammed in the sub-zero temperatures. Optics fogged. Vehicles could only be started by lighting a fire beneath them to liquefy lubricants that had become tar-like in the cold. In contrast, the Red Army's tank were suited to winter warfare with their broad tracks and diesel engines, while the Soviet infantry was well-equipped with snowsuits, warm clothing and reliable weapons.

Although the succeeding winters were not so harsh and the Germans were better equipped for them, the approach of winter was anticipated with dread every year.

THE GREAT PATRIOTIC WAR

'Eternal glory to the heroes who fell in the struggle for freedom for our country ... Death to the German invaders.' – Stalin announcing the liberation of Belgorod in August 1943. Stalin used the closing phrase 'Death to the German invaders' in every subsequent victory announcement – more than 300 times before the end of the Great Patriotic War.

The Eastern Front was the site of the largest and most intensive military operations of World War II and, for that matter, in the entirety of human history. It was also the most savage. 80% of Germany's casualties were suffered in the east – more than four million men. Even such dreadful numbers are dwarfed by those suffered by the Soviet Union – 26.6 million dead, more than half of them civilians. For the Germans the *Ostfront* was to be an ideological war between two totalitarian regimes and Hitler made it known from the outset that the Soviet Union was not only to be conquered, but its people enslaved and exterminated. To the Soviets it became 'the Great Patriotic War' – a fight not over warring ideologies but for the very survival of their Motherland and its peoples.

1941 – MOSCOW

On 22 June 1941 Germany invaded the Soviet Union, crossing the border with 99 divisions, 14 of them Panzer. Incredibly, Stalin seems to have been genuinely surprised by the move (much like the Americans at Pearl Harbor), having resolutely ignored all the warning signs. In fact Stalin and his cronies did much to contribute to the lack of readiness in the border forces through fear of giving 'provocation' to the Germans. It turned out that the Germans needed no such excuse.

The Soviet border forces were swept away like 'a row of glass houses' as armoured spearheads lunged deep into the rear. The fast-moving Panzers encircled hundreds of thousands of Red Army soldiers as they struggled to concentrate and fight back under the incessant lash of the Luftwaffe. The slower moving German infantry set about destroying the trapped pockets as the Panzers raced onward to new objectives. Within weeks the Germans had thrust hundreds of kilometres into Belorussia and the Ukraine. Within months they stood at the very gates of Moscow.

But in their overconfidence the Germans had miscalculated. They expected the Soviet Union to collapse like France had done after a brief Blitzkrieg campaign and were astonished by the continuous, seemingly hopeless, resistance they encountered.

Defenders of Stalingrad (L–R): anti-tank rifleman, submachine gunner, tanker, by Ronald Volstad © Osprey Publishing Ltd. Taken from Men-at-Arms 216: The Red Army of the Great Patriotic War 1941–45.

On Hitler's orders the Panzers had diverted their efforts to capture the Soviet Union's main resource and industrial areas, even as the Soviets frantically disassembled their factories and sent them eastwards out of reach. Now time had run out and the full weight of the Russian winter descended on the ill-prepared German armies as they struggled towards the Soviet capital.

1942 – STALINGRAD

The Soviet winter counter-offensive caught the Germans by surprise as it seemed inconceivable that the Red Army was still capable of mounting an offensive after the losses it had suffered. The frozen, exhausted German army wavered and almost collapsed before the onslaught. Hitler sacked his high command and took charge of the army himself, ordering that there be no retreat and that every position must be fought 'to the last bullet'. By so doing the Germans avoided the fate of Napoleon's army, torn to pieces in the retreat from Moscow, but the affair reinforced Hitler's notions of his own military genius in a way that would eventually cost Germany dear.

Stalin, too, had a part to play in making matters worse for the soldiers on the front lines. By insisting on wide ranging counter-offensives he squandered the already overextended forces of the Red Army, ensuring that in the summer the Germans could once again seize the initiative. In 1942 the Panzers drove forward in the south of the country, with Hitler's eyes once again fixed on capturing more resources to feed the Nazi war machine. The German armies reached their high water mark at the city of Stalingrad, in a battle that came to symbolise the struggle between Hitler and Stalin.

The Germans failed to take Stalingrad in months of bloody street-fighting. The city was reduced to rubble and its population decimated, but the Red Army fought on among the ruins in what the Germans called 'Rattenkrieg' – the war of the rats. As winter descended the Soviets counterattacked again, this time with greater numbers and better coordination than at Moscow. The German troops at Stalingrad were cut off and forced to surrender in the biggest defeat yet suffered by Hitler's Third Reich. The front lines were again pushed west by the Soviets but, once again, they bent and did not break, while the over-ambitious Red Army pushed too far and was punished for its temerity at Kharkov by the veteran German Heer.

'IVAN'

'Even those of who knew that our government was wicked, that there was little to choose between the SS and the NKVD except their language, and who despised the hypocrisy of Communist politics –we felt that we must fight. Because every Russian who had lived through the Revolution and the thirties had felt a breeze of hope, for the first time in the history of our people. We were like the bud at the tip of a root, which has wound its way for centuries under rocky soil. We felt ourselves to be within inches of the open sky. We knew that we would die, of course. But our children would inherit two things: A land free of the invader; and Time, in which the progressive ideals of Communism might emerge.'

The German trooper's opponent on the Eastern Front was 'Ivan', the archetypal Red Army soldier. Ivan was tough and tenacious (particularly in defence) but also volatile and wildly unpredictable. At times he was found to be patient and enduring beyond imagination, capable of lying motionless in the snow for hours, exposed to the full blast of winter weather while awaiting the order to attack. At other times Ivan would charge wildly into battle, hurling himself into the maw of the guns with suicidal recklessness.

The Germans found Ivan to be brave and courageous in some instances, and a contemptible coward in others. On occasion, Soviet units that had driven back the Germans with ferocious courage would suddenly flee in panic from a small assault group attacking on an unexpected axis. Whole battalions might lose their nerve when the first shot was fired, but the same battalions would fight with fanatical stubbornness the next day.

Wounded or unconscious men would reach for their weapons the moment they regained consciousness, even the crews of burning tanks would keep shooting while there was still breath in their bodies.

Ivan was capable of operations regardless of the season or environment, was an expert at infiltrating German lines and capable of sustaining himself with only a fraction of the supplies needed by Western armies. Given a hatchet and a knife he could rapidly furnish himself with shelter, food and transport, even in the depths of winter, by living off the land. Meanwhile, German troops shivered in villages and burned their remaining supplies of fuel just to keep warm.

Red Army soldiers were reputed to 'dig like moles'. Given half a chance they quickly vanished into slit trenches and gun pits skilfully positioned to take advantage of the terrain. The German doctrine of making rapid counter-attacks to take back lost ground became an obsession on the Eastern Front. With minutes Ivan would be dug in and twice as hard to evict. Within hours he would have mines, tanks and guns emplaced to protect his gains.

As Ivan became better equipped he became a real threat, and eventually something of a bogeyman for the Germans. The wasteful human wave tactics of the early war were gradually discarded. The Red Army began to fight tactically, constantly working to gain the dominant ground with coordinated fire support from artillery, mortars and tanks. Infiltration and reconnaissance became Ivan's key skills at the tactical level as the war progressed, although the cruder 'Soviet steamroller' always stood ready to crush a determined defence.

T-34/76 and tank riders

1943 – KURSK

By 1943 it was apparent that the Germans had 'caught a wolf by the ears' and could not afford to let go. The Red Army was becoming stronger and more experienced every year while German strength was ebbing away. The Western Allies were applying more pressure against Occupied Europe and although the much-demanded 'second front' had finally been opened in Africa, it had little impact on the war in the east. The Germans decided to strike in the summer with the aim of destroying as much of the Soviet mobile forces as possible, thereby taking the sting of the following winter's counter-offensive. The stage was being set for the biggest armoured battle of the war.

For their part, the Red Army leadership (Stalin having learned to take a back seat in military planning by this time) recognised the German threat and prepared for it by digging in around the city of Kursk. The Blitzkrieg had never failed yet and the Soviets had yet to defeat the German Heer in summer time, but now they felt confident. When the Germans attacked in mid-summer, their new generation of Panzers was grinding its way into a heavily guarded maze of minefields, trenches and tank traps. Only when the Panzer spearheads were blunted did the Red Army commit its own tank forces *en masse* to complete the Germans' defeat. Over 3,000 tanks met in the battle of Kursk, and when the smoke cleared it was the Germans that were in retreat. The Blitzkrieg had been broken.

After Kursk the war in the east became one of German retreat and Soviet advance. There were holding actions and counter-attacks, but the movement was inexorably westward.

Soviet infantry advance alongside an SU-76

The Soviet advance on Kahnsfelde, by Peter Dennis © Osprey Publishing Ltd. Taken from Duel 37: King Tiger vs IS-2.

1944-45 – BERLIN

By 1944 even the most fanatical Nazis could see that the war in the east had become unwinnable. The Red Army pushed back the Germans further and further, ousting them from territories occupied in 1941–42 before driving into Poland and then Germany itself. Now it was the turn of the Germans to fight in a fanatical, hopeless defence of their homeland. Hemmed in on all sides by a rising tide of enemies, the Germans feared the approach of the 'Asiatic hordes' from the east most of all.

A last, desperate defence was thrown up at Berlin as the Red Army closed in with overwhelming numbers. The Germans managed to inflict heavy casualties on the Soviets (as they always did) but it availed them nothing. Adolf Hitler committed suicide as Red Army shells rained down around his bunker and Berlin itself suffered the fate it had imposed on so many other capitals. The war in Europe was at an end.

ARMY LIST

The liberation of the Peterhof, by Peter Dennis © Osprey Publishing Ltd. Taken from Campaign 215: Leningrad 1941–44.

This Army List is based on the troops and equipment available to the Soviet forces from the German invasion in 1941 until the surrender of Berlin in May 1945. Four years of incessant conflict forced the Red Army to rapidly evolve from a poorly trained, led and equipped fighting force into a modern, mechanised army forged in battle. The privations of the war meant that Soviet forces were often equipped only with the bare necessities to fight. In the first years even rifles and ammunition were in short supply but, as the war continued, the Red Army repeatedly astonished its opponents with the number of tanks, planes and – most of all – artillery pieces it could bring to bear through relentless prioritization of production. Soviet equipment was rugged and practical, built to endure the harsh Russian winters and the handling of barely trained Russian troops. It included what was probably the best all-round tank of the war – the T-34. The Russians also possessed some of the most effective artillery of the war, including long-ranged guns and the notorious multiple-rocket launcher known to the Germans as 'Stalin's organ'.

This is the official Bolt Action Army List for the forces of Soviet Russia and its allies in World War II. This fuller and more detailed listing both augments and supersedes the shorter Army List included in the Bolt Action rulebook.

Players can pick an army in either of two ways:

- Use the Reinforced Platoon list from the Bolt Action rulebook in conjunction with the Army List in this book. To save referencing back to the rulebook, the generic Reinforced Platoon selector is repeated below.
- Instead of using the generic Reinforced Platoon list, use any one of the Theatre Selectors on page 62–86 in conjunction with the Army List given in this book.

Either method is perfectly acceptable depending on what kind of game you wish to play. The first method uses the generic selector and is more flexible and therefore ideal for pick-up games against any opponent, as it allows for a wider variety of different kinds of troops and equipment. The second

The Black Death close in for the kill

82mm medium mortar team

method using the Theatre Selectors is more historically representative and therefore better suited for games where a historical portrayal is envisaged; for example a stubborn defence among the fortified districts during the early phases of Operation *Barbarossa*, a street battle in Stalingrad or the final drive into East Prussia. We imagine that players will, on the whole, prefer to fight battles within a specific historical

context, in which case simply use the appropriate Theatre Selector to choose your army.

REINFORCED PLATOON

1 Lieutenant – First or Second
2 Infantry squads

plus:

0–3 Infantry squads
0–1 Captain or Major
0–1 Medic
0–1 Forward Observer (either Artillery or Air)
0–1 Machine gun team
0–1 Mortar team
0–1 Sniper team
0–1 Flamethrower team
0–1 Anti-tank team
0–1 Field Artillery, Anti-aircraft or Anti-tank gun
0–1 Armoured Car
0–1 Tank, Tank Destroyer, Anti-aircraft vehicle or Self-propelled Artillery
0–1 Transport vehicle or tow (soft skins or armoured) **per** infantry and artillery unit in the reinforced platoon.

Note that the generic Reinforced Platoon does not include provision for a commissar. This is because the commissar is a uniquely Russian officer while the generic Reinforced Platoon is the common selector for all armies. If a commissar is required he can be included in the generic Reinforced Platoon under the 'Captain or Major' slot. So, 0–1 Captain, Major or Commissar can be included in a generic Soviet Reinforced Platoon.

Soviet M5 half-track

Occupiers of Berlin (L–R): anti-tank grenadier, junior lieutenant of artillery, NKVD Internal Security Officer, by Ronald Volstad © Osprey Publishing Ltd. Taken from Men-at-Arms 216: The Red Army of the Great Patriotic War 1941–45.

ARMY SPECIAL RULES

THE GREAT PATRIOTIC WAR

Throughout the war Russian forces endured a rate of casualties unimaginable in the west and which would undoubtedly have broken a people less inured to hardship and sacrifice.

Whenever a unit of infantry or artillery models fails a morale check and would otherwise be destroyed as a consequence, take the test again and apply this second result. This re-roll applies to all infantry and artillery units, including HQ units, facing this situation. Note that this rule only applies to infantry and artillery, and not to tanks or other vehicles.

QUANTITY HAS A QUALITY ALL OF ITS OWN

'If you have more men than they have bullets, they will eventually run out of ammunition.'

To represent the vast manpower available within the Soviet Union, the force may include a free twelve-man strong Rifle Squad of Inexperienced infantry equipped with all the options available to them. This free squad is in addition to units chosen from whatever Selector is used. See the Rifle Squad entry on page 23.

NOT ONE STEP BACK!

Soviet armies can include commissars as noted in the relevant selectors. Commissars are political officers and do not confer a Morale bonus to nearby troops. If soldiers show signs of disobeying orders the commissars will not hesitate to shoot them. When a friendly infantry unit fails an Order test within 6'' of a commissar, remove one model from the unit and re-roll the dice. Note that there is no choice in the matter – if the commissar is within 6" of the unit he will shoot dissenters whether you want him to or not! The second result stands as normal – the commissar can only make a single re-roll for each unit affected. This rule does not apply to units other than infantry, and does not apply to infantry units already reduced to one or two models, or consisting of only one or two models to start with (in the case of some teams for example).

MASSED BATTERIES

The Soviets excelled in their use of massed artillery and Red Army artillery barrages were truly terrifying. Therefore we give a bonus to the Soviet artillery barrage. When rolling to determine the 'Fire for effect' radius from the aiming point (D6+6") instead of rolling one die roll two dice and take the highest score. For example, if you roll a 2 and a 5 the roll of 5 is used, so units within 5+6=11" of the aiming point will be hit by the barrage. See the Bolt Action rulebook, page 64.

TYPES OF UNIT

The list is divided into categories as follows.

1 Infantry	Headquarters units
	Infantry squads and teams
2 Artillery	Field artillery
	Anti-tank guns
3 Vehicles	Tanks
	Tank destroyers
	Self-propelled artillery
	Anti-aircraft vehicles
	Armoured cars
	Transports and tows

INFANTRY

HEADQUARTERS UNITS

Each platoon is built upon a core that includes a headquarters unit in the form of a Senior or Junior Lieutenant (the Russian equivalents to First and Second Lieutenant). Other HQ units can be added to the force, including higher-ranking officers, as well as medical units and supporting observers.

OFFICER

Like the soldiers they commanded, many Soviet officers were inexperienced and lacked training at the beginning of the Great Patriotic War. Stalin's ruthless purge of the officers of the Red Army in 1937 had denuded the organization of leadership and left deep scars in the survivors' minds. Throughout the war, showing initiative was seen as a dangerous trait, and most Soviet officers would follow their orders to the letter even if they meant marching their men to certain death. Soviet operational

leadership improved immeasurably over time, but the heavy casualties endured by the Red Army indicates that overall battlefield control remained a blunt instrument. A great reliance was placed on forward planning, timetables and pre-set objectives to overcome shortcomings. An officer unit consists of the officer himself and can include up to two other men acting as his immediate attendants. Soviet officers can be rated as Inexperienced, Regular or Veteran.

Cost: Second (Junior) Lieutenant 35pts (Inexperienced),
   50pts (Regular), 65pts (Veteran)
First (Senior) Lieutenant 60pts (Inexperienced), 75pts (Regular),
   90pts (Veteran)
Captain 95pts (Inexperienced), 110pts (Regular), 125pts (Veteran)
Major 135pts (Inexperienced), 150pts (Regular), 165pts (Veteran)
Team: 1 officer and up to 2 further men
Weapons: Pistol, submachine gun, or rifle as depicted on the
   models
Options:
- The officer may be accompanied by up to 2 men at a cost of +7pts per man (Inexperienced), +10pts per man (Regular) or +13pts per man (Veteran)

COMMISSAR

At various times from its formation during the Revolution, the Red Army included a *Politruk* – a political commissar. Politruks were Communist Party members charged with educating the troops

and monitoring their officers for signs of counter-revolutionary ideology. They were placed within the command structure in every unit down to company level and reported to Revolutionary Military Councils (RVS) that were established at Army level. The office of political commissars was instituted from 1919–24, from 1937–40, and again from 1941–42, forming a dual-command system that often had disastrous consequences. While Politruks tirelessly rooted out shirkers, defeatists and cowards, many innocent men were also executed out of hand, or sent to punishment battalions thanks to their efforts. A commissar unit consists of the commissar himself and can include up to two other (politically reliable) men. Commissars are rated as Inexperienced. Note that, if you choose a Soviet army using the generic Platoon Selector you can take a Commissar instead of a Major or Captain, as already explained in the introductory section. In other selectors commissars are indicated separately.

Cost: 15pts (Inexperienced)
Team: 1 commissar and up to 2 further men
Weapons: Pistol, submachine gun, or rifle as depicted on the
   models
Options:
- The commissar may be accompanied by up to 2 men at a cost of +7pts per man
Special Rules:
- Not one step back! (see page 21)

MEDIC

The field medic presents the wounded soldier with his best chance of surviving serious injury and can ensure that lightly wounded soldiers are returned to fighting fitness as rapidly as possible. In the Soviet army the medics were commonly young women who, although not intended for frontline service, were repeatedly recorded as risking their lives to rescue wounded comrades. The men of the Red army had a healthy respect for these angels of mercy.

Cost: Medic 25pts (Regular), 30pts (Veteran)
Team: 1 medic and up to 2 further men/women
Weapons: Pistol or none, as depicted on the model

SOVIET WOMEN IN WORLD WAR II

According to the writings of Karl Marx and Lenin, Communism fully embraced the concept of equal rights without regard to gender. In practice this ideal was not heavily pursued, but in comparison to the rest of the world in the 1930s the Soviet Union was still extremely progressive in its thinking on equality. When the Germans invaded, thousands of women volunteered for the armed forces, but were initially turned away. As the dreadful casualties of the first year of war mounted and influential women campaigned for their right to fight for their country, official policy shifted. By the end of the Great Patriotic War, 800,000 women served in the Soviet armed forces, 200,000 of whom were decorated – 89 of these were awards of the Hero of the Soviet Union.

Women served as pilots, mechanics, tankers, medics, gunners, partisans, snipers, political officers and communication personnel. Three air regiments were formed entirely of female recruits and produced the world's only female fighter aces, Lydia Litvyak (12 kills) and Katya Budanov (11 kills). Arguably the most famous of all were the Red Army's female snipers, such as Nina Alexeyevna Lobkovskaya, who commanded a company of female snipers in the battle for Berlin, and Lyudmila Pavlichenko who killed 309 in the fighting at Odessa and Sevastopol in the first years of the war.

The Germans seem to have been particularly upset by fighting female soldiers, as it appears to have clashed badly with their chivalric fantasies of being a 'civilising' force. The Soviets found such squeamishness bizarre, given the lack of compunction shown by German pilots about bombing or strafing civilian women and children, or the German Heer's attempts to starve the inhabitants of Leningrad to death.

Options:
- The medic may be accompanied by up to 2 men/women at a cost of +10pts (Regular) or +13pts (Veteran) each

FORWARD OBSERVER

Forward observers are liaison officers responsible for coordinating the attack of heavy artillery, rocket batteries or aircraft strikes. Soviet aviation was utterly ravaged in the first weeks of the invasion, but persisted in making attacks with what was described as 'mulish obstinacy' as it rebuilt itself into a substantial threat over the following years. Soviet artillery deployment was crude but highly effective and left a lasting impression on the soldiers of the *Ostheer*. Forward observers are likely to be accompanied by a field telephone or radio operator and other immediate attendants. We rate these officers as Regular or Veteran.

Cost: Artillery Forward Observer 100pts (Regular), 115pts (Veteran)
Air Force Forward Observer 75pts (Regular), 90pts (Veteran)
Team: 1 Forward Observer and up to 2 further men
Weapons: Pistol, submachine gun, or rifle as depicted on the models
Options:
- The observer may be accompanied by up to 2 men at a cost of +10pts per man (Regular) or +13pts per man (Veteran)

Special Rules:
- Massed batteries (Artillery Forward Observer, see page 21)

INFANTRY SQUADS & TEAMS

The Red Army was vast, fielding over 34 million soldiers in the Great Patriotic War, of whom almost a third were destined to give their lives defending the Motherland. The Russian foot soldier has long been celebrated for his ability to endure the worst that the enemy, the Russian winter, and his own superiors can throw at him. As in all armies there were elite fighting formations as well as scratch units trained in only the most basic way, but because of the sheer size of the Red Army the latter always tended to outnumber the former. Still, the Red Army of the late war was not the disorganised and poorly led force that the Germans had so easily defeated in 1941 – even if its chief advantage was still one of numbers rather than quality.

RIFLE SQUAD

On 24 July 1941 new organizational tables were issued for 'reduced strength' infantry divisions that gave mute testimony to the scale of losses in just a few weeks of war with Germany. The hopeless battles on the frontier and before Smolensk had destroyed so much materiel that infantry battalions had their heavy weapons inventory ruthlessly slashed. On paper, each platoon was allocated only two light machine guns so some squads had to go into battle armed only with rifles. Even submachine guns were reserved for specialist companies formed at regimental level. Later in the war pure rifle squads became far less commonplace as Soviet factories relocated east and restarted production. Note that a Soviet army is allowed to field an additional 12-man Inexperienced Rifle Squad for free to represent the advantage of numbers. This free unit is in addition to any units chosen from whatever selector is used, and is equipped with all available options (anti-tank grenades).

Red Army rifle squad

Cost: Inexperienced Infantry 35pts
Composition: 1 NCO and 4 men
Weapons: Rifles
Options:
- Add up to 7 additional soldiers with rifles at +7pts each
- The entire squad may have anti-tank grenades (Molotov cocktails) for +2pts per model

Special Rules:
- *Green*
- Tank hunters (if anti-tank grenades taken)

LIGHT MACHINE GUN SQUAD

At the opening of Operation *Barbarossa* in 1941 the basic Russian infantry squad consisted of ten men led by a sergeant and a junior sergeant – the Russian equivalent of a corporal. Each squad included a light machine gun and one of the ordinary squad members would act as its loader – this would usually be the DP (*Degtyaryov Pekhotny*) machine gun, nicknamed the 'record player' for its distinctive round pan magazine. Wartime shortages meant the DP machine gun was often replaced with the more compact DT tank light machine gun or even captured German machine guns. The rest of the unit carried either bolt action or semi-automatic rifles and all would carry grenades. In July 1942 the standard squad size was reduced to two sergeants and seven men while the number of light machine guns available per platoon was increased to six, allowing two squads to be armed with two light machine guns. In late August 1943 squad size was changed again to one sergeant and ten privates, the increase being 'paid for' by basic platoons being reduced to having three squads instead of four. Note that because of this variable organisation the number of light machine guns available to a squad is limited to one in the Theatre Selectors for pre-July 1942 units and for additional units thereafter.

A light machine gunner keeps the enemy pinned down

SPECIAL RULE: BODY ARMOUR

The Red Army used several types of body armour, but only the SN-42 (*'Stalynoi Nagrudnik'* – 'steel breastplate', design year 1942) appears to have been put into large-scale production. It consisted of two pressed steel plates that protected the front of the torso and groin. The plates were 2 mm thick and weighed 3.5kg (7.7lbs). This armour was supplied to assault engineers and to the tank riders of some tank brigades. The SN armour protected wearers from 9mm bullets fired by an MP40 at around 100 meters, which made it useful in urban fighting such as the battle of Stalingrad. However, the SN's weight made it impractical for infantry in the open.

Small arms (rifles, machine guns, etc.) and HE suffer a -1 modifier to damage soldiers wearing body armour.

Troops wearing body armour do not increase their pace when given a run order. They can still be given a run order (to assault an enemy in close combat for example) but don't move any faster: they run at the normal pace of 6".

Cost: Inexperienced Infantry 35pts or Regular Infantry 50pts
Composition: 1 NCO and 4 men
Weapons: Rifles
Options:
- Add up to 7 additional soldiers with rifles at +7pts each (Inexperienced) or +10pts each (Regular)
- The NCO may have a submachine gun instead of a rifle for +3pts
- Up to two soldiers may have a LMG for +20pts each – for each LMG included another man becomes the loader
- The entire squad may have anti-tank grenades for +2pts per model

Special Rules:
- Tank hunters (if anti-tank grenades taken)

SUBMACHINE GUN SQUAD

Experiences in the Finnish campaign in 1939–40 convinced the Soviets of the value of submachine guns and led to the adoption of the excellent Shpagin PPSh design with its distinctive drum magazine. The PPSh suited the Red Army soldier perfectly as it was cheap, robust and easy to use. The PPSh and the later PPS model proved extremely popular. Russian industry produced over six million submachine guns (34% of total small arms production), compared to Germany producing just over a million (11% of their small arms production). Dedicated submachine gun-armed companies were formed at Regimental level and deployed for shock assaults, trench and street fighting.

Cost: Inexperienced Infantry 50pts or Regular Infantry 65pts
Composition: 1 NCO and 4 men
Weapons: Submachine guns
Options:
- Add up to 7 additional soldiers with SMGs at +10pts each (Inexperienced) or +13pts each (Regular)
- One soldier may have a LMG for +20pts. Another soldier becomes the loader
- The entire squad may have anti-tank grenades for +2pts per model

Special Rules:
- Tank hunters (if anti-tank grenades taken)

TANK RIDERS SQUAD

Soviet tank units were commonly paired with *tankodesantniki* – submachine gun-armed troops assigned the unenviable task of riding the tanks into battle to defend them from enemy infantry. The Red Army did not build armoured personnel carriers of its own like the German Sdkfz 251 or the US M3 halftrack, and there were precious few trucks available, so Red Army soldiers commonly rode into battle on tanks. As Soviet mechanised formations took to the offensive, this arrangement was formalised and dedicated infantry units were included in the table of organization for the purpose. Veteran Soviet tank crews developed a close bond with their tankodesantniki as their 'eyes and ears', and the pairing formed an effective combined-arms unit.

Cost: Regular Infantry 65pts or Veteran Infantry 80pts
Composition: 1 NCO and 4 men
Weapons: Submachine guns
Options:
- Add up o 6 additional soldiers with submachine guns at +13pts each (Regular) or +16pts each (Veteran)
- One soldier may have a LMG for +20pts. Another soldier becomes the loader
- The entire squad may have anti-tank grenades for +2pts per model
- The entire squad may have SN-42 body armour for +5pts per model

Special Rules:
- Tank hunters (if anti-tank grenades taken)
- Tank Riders: A tank rider unit can mount onto or dismount from a tank counting it as a transport for these purposes. Once mounted the unit is replaced by a few tank rider models placed on the tank itself. One unit of tank riders can ride upon one tank. As with other transported units the tank riders cannot be targeted whilst they ride upon their tank; however, unlike with other transported troops, tank riders must immediately disembark if the tank they are riding upon is shot at.

Regardless of what kind of weapon is shooting at the tank, so long as the firer is within range of the tank the tank rider unit immediately disembarks when the shot is declared and before rolling dice to determine hits. Units disembarking in this way immediately go 'down' or remain 'down' if they are down already.

T-34/76 and tank riders

GUARDS SQUAD

In the Red Army the Guards honorific was awarded to units proven in combat and would therefore tend to denote elite troops. They were certainly given priority when it came to supplies, promotion and access to automatic weapons. They were also given the toughest assignments, often resulting in such a rate of attrition that by the end of the war many Guards units consisted mostly of raw recruits. We shall even this variation out by giving 'ordinary' Guards Regular status. Note that the number of light machine guns available to a squad is limited to one in the Theatre Selectors for pre-July 1942 units and for additional units thereafter, as already described for light machine gun squads.

Cost: Regular Infantry 50pts
Composition: 1 NCO and 4 men
Weapons: Rifles
Options:
- Add up to 6 additional soldiers with rifles at +10pts each.
- Any soldiers may have a submachine gun instead of a rifle for +3pts each
- Up two soldiers may have a LMG for +20pts each – for each LMG included another man becomes the loader
- One soldier can have a (captured) panzerfaust in addition to other weapons for +5pts
- The entire squad may have anti-tank grenades for +2pts per model

Special Rules:
- Tank hunters (if anti-tank grenades taken)

VETERAN SQUADS

Such was the intensity of the fighting on the eastern front that a soldier could be considered a veteran after his first battle. In the battle of Stalingrad soldiers were considered alumni of the 'Stalingrad Academy of Street Fighting' if they survived the Volga crossing and made it as far as the front lines just a few hundred yards from the shore. If the Soviet army was not on the whole an elite fighting force, it certainly included its fair share of battle-hardened veterans. It was not uncommon for squads of hand-picked, decorated men to be assigned to particularly important objectives or critical areas where their greater experience would have the most impact. Red

Army soldiers took great pride in being recognised for their bravery and those awarded with the highest Soviet medal – 'Hero of the Soviet Union' – were truly worthy of the epithet. The veteran squad represented here might be used for either veteran Guards or ordinary infantry formations depending on the theatre and date. Note that the number of light machine guns available to a squad is limited to one in the Theatre Selectors for pre-July 1942 units and for additional units thereafter, as already described for light machine gun squads.

Cost: Veteran Infantry 65pts
Composition: 1 NCO and 4 men
Weapons: Rifles
Options:
- Add up to 6 additional soldiers at +13pts each
- Any soldiers may have a submachine gun instead of a rifle for +3pts each
- Up two soldiers may have a LMG for +20pts each – for each LMG included another man becomes the loader
- Up to two soldiers can have a (captured) panzerfaust in addition to other weapons for +5pts each
- The entire squad may have anti-tank grenades for +2pts per model
- Any veterans squad can be *Tough Fighters* for +1pts per man

Special Rules:
- Tank hunters (if anti-tank grenades taken)
- *Tough Fighters* (if option is taken)

NKVD SQUADS

In 1941 the Soviet Union's fortified borders were manned by units of the NKVD (People's Commissariat for Internal Affairs). These units were almost entirely destroyed in the first weeks of the campaign. After this, NKVD troops were chiefly used for internal security, but could potentially fight on the frontline as they did at Stalingrad in 1942 and during the Crimean Offensive in 1944. In the normal course of operations NKVD troops set up 'blocking positions' just behind the battle line to turn back fleeing troops with machine gun fire if necessary. NKVD checkpoints at bridges and road junctions monitored all traffic behind the front and were sometimes disguised as bridge-building crews or road repair gangs to catch out unauthorised movements. In 1943 the SMERSH (acronym from the Russian for 'Death to Spies') agency was formed as a distinct branch of the NKVD to carry out these tasks.

Cost: Regular Infantry 50pts
Composition: 1 NCO and 4 men
Weapons: Rifles
Options:
- Add up to 6 additional soldiers with rifles at +10pts each.
- Any soldiers may have a submachine gun instead of a rifle for +3pts each
- One soldier may have a LMG for +20pts. Another soldier becomes the loader
- NKVD Squads can be *Fanatics* at +3pts per man

Special Rules:
- *Fanatics* (if option is taken)

SHTRAFBAT SQUAD

In July 1942 Stalin issued Order No. 227, popularised as the 'not one step back!' (*Ni Shagu Nazad!*) order. The order included severe punishments for unauthorised retreat and made provision for the creation of punishment units patterned after the Wehrmacht *Strafbattalions*. The Shtrafbat were penal battalions formed from troops accused of cowardice or desertion, or from civilian (often political) prisoners, or from ex-prisoners of war who stood accused of treason for having allowed themselves to be captured by the enemy. The maximum sentence in a penal battalion was limited to three months. Although in theory an individual could redeem his status by some act of heroism on the battlefield, in practice this was unlikely and service in the Shtrafbat was commonly considered equivalent to a death sentence. '*Shtrafniks*' were often used to draw enemy fire, or to expose enemy positions by advancing into them, and some were employed as 'tramplers' – human mine clearers (those closest to completing their sentence commonly drew this duty). Penal units were not always armed or might carry dummy weapons, but were usually fortified with large quantities of Vodka.

Cost: Inexperienced Infantry 35pts
Composition: 1 NCO and 4 men
Weapons: Rifles
Options:
- Add up to 7 additional unarmed men at 4pts each
- Any unarmed men may be given rifles at +3pts each
- Shtrafbat units can be *Shirkers* for a reduction of 3pts per man

Special Rules:
- *Shirkers* (if option is taken)
- Unarmed men neither shoot nor attack in close quarters – their only value is as casualties

CAVALRY SQUAD

An anachronism to Western eyes by the start of World War II, horsed cavalry formations remained in the Soviet order of battle until 1955. The vast open spaces of continental Russia contained many regions where vehicles, even tanks, could not operate off-road but cavalry could roam at will – especially during winter and the spring thaw. Between July and December 1941 no fewer than 78 cavalry divisions and three mountain cavalry divisions were formed. Stavka continued to progressively expand and strengthen the cavalry formations throughout the war, with an increasing complement of machine guns, mortars and anti-aircraft weapons. Although the Cossacks had been heavily repressed for their support of the counter-revolutionary White Russians during the Civil War, some were 'persuaded' to serve as cavalry in the Red Army (others chose to serve the Germans). A large number of horsed formations were also raised in Central Asia, including five Uzbek cavalry divisions. Cavalry normally used their horses only for transport and fought on foot, but more than one surprised German unit found itself the object of an old-fashioned cavalry charge!

Cost: Regular Infantry 50pts
Composition: 1 NCO and 4 men
Weapons: Cavalry carbines (see below)
Options:
- Add up to 5 additional men with carbines at +10pts each
- Any soldiers may have a submachine gun instead of a carbine for +3pts each
- One soldier may have a LMG for +20pts. Another soldier becomes the loader
- The entire squad may be mounted upon horses for +2pts per man
- Cavalry Squads can be *Tough Fighters* at +1pts per man

Special Rules:
- *Tough Fighters* (if option is taken)
- A mounted squad uses the *Cavalry* rules (Bolt Action rulebook, page 71)
- Cavalry Carbines: Carbines count as pistols when used from horseback, and rifles when used on foot

PEOPLE'S MILITIA SQUAD

'Popular regimentation' or the 'people's volunteer militia' (*Narodnoe Opolcheniye* or *Opolchenie*) is a Russian tradition dating back to the 16th century and a powerful part of the national heritage. In times of emergency, a militia was selected from volunteers to serve alongside the regular army and defend their homes. In the dark days of 1941–42, workers and citizens in Leningrad, Moscow, Rostov, Stalingrad and other major Soviet cities organised into militias and quickly found themselves on the front lines as the fascist invaders swept east. People's militia squads were even more poorly trained and equipped than the average Red Army squad, but they fought on with tragic bravery.

Cost: Inexperienced Infantry 35pts
Composition: 1 NCO and 4 men
Weapons: Rifles
Options:

- Add up to 7 additional unarmed men at 4pts each
- Any unarmed men may be given rifles at +3pts each
- The entire squad may have anti-tank grenades (Molotov cocktails) for +2pts per model

Special Rules:

- *Green*
- Tank hunters (if anti-tank grenades taken)
- Unarmed men neither shoot nor attack in close quarters – their only value is as casualties

SIBERIAN SQUAD

By December 1941 Stalin became confident that the Japanese would not dare to attack the Soviet Union in the Far East. Divisions of crack Siberian troops were moved westward and concentrated around Moscow to prepare for the winter counter-offensive. These soldiers had been hardened in border conflicts with the Japanese Imperial Army. For the Germans, shivering at the end of tenuous supply lines, the unexpected appearance of the tough, well-equipped Siberians became symbolic of the 'vast Asiatic hordes' that remained undefeated in the east.

Cost: Regular Infantry 55pts or Veteran Infantry 70pts
Composition: 1 NCO and 4 men
Weapons: Rifles
Options:

- Add up to 7 additional soldiers at +11pts each (Regular) or +14pts each (Veteran)
- Any soldiers may have a submachine gun instead of a rifle for +3pts each
- One soldier may have a LMG for +20pts. Another soldier becomes the loader
- The entire squad may have anti-tank grenades for +2pts per model
- Any Siberians squad can be *Tough Fighters* for +1pts per man

Special Rules:

- Tank hunters (if anti-tank grenades taken)
- *Tough Fighters* (if option is taken)

SKI TROOPS SQUAD

As the Wehrmacht ground to a halt at the gates of Moscow in the depths of the Russian winter Soviet ski troops became a

particular terror for them. Swift and silent as ghosts in their white camouflage smocks, ski troops could strike and then withdraw across the deep snow that paralysed all other combatants. Surprisingly the Red Army had no ski troops of its own in 1939. Rough handling by Finnish ski troops during the 1939–40 Winter War underlined their value to Red Army generals and a number of scratch ski battalions were put together from available personnel. In the winter of 1941 the Soviets raised nearly 300 ski battalions and formed several into brigades on the Karelian Front. Ski troops were seen as seasonal units so they were raised and disbanded each winter.

Red Army ski troops, by Peter Dennis © Osprey Publishing Ltd. Taken from Elite 156: World War II Combat Reconnaissance Tactics.

Cost: Regular Infantry 55pts or Veteran Infantry 70pts
Composition: 1 NCO and 4 men
Weapons: Rifles
Options:

- Add up to 7 additional soldiers at +11pts each (Regular) or +14pts each (Veteran)
- Any soldiers may have a submachine gun instead of a rifle for +3pts each
- One soldier may have a LMG for +20pts. Another soldier becomes the loader
- The entire squad may have anti-tank grenades for +2pts per model

Special Rules:

- Tank hunters (if anti-tank grenades taken)
- Ski troops ignore movement penalties for snow and other winter conditions

AIRBORNE SQUAD

The Soviets were visionaries in the development of airborne troops and tactics, first forming a brigade-sized airborne unit after successful trials in December 1932. More units followed and by June 1941 five Airborne Corps existed in the Soviet order of battle, undoubtedly the strongest airborne force in the world. However in the desperate fighting of the early campaign these formations were pressed into service as regular infantry and virtually consumed. Airborne troops were finally dropped in battalion strength during the defence of Moscow during December 1941 and January 1942. An entire corps (the 4th) was dropped operationally in February 1942 but while it survived for six months in the German rear, it failed to achieve its objectives. The crisis at Stalingrad then pulled in all available airborne troops to fight as regular infantry again. The last major Soviet airborne operation was an attempt to seize bridgeheads on the west bank of the Dnepr with two corps in September 1943, which proved to be a debacle of such poor planning that it was doomed from the start. Soviet airborne troops always fought with tremendous courage and élan, but lacked heavy anti-tank weapons and were badly supported in every operation they attempted.

Cost: Veteran Infantry 65pts
Composition: 1 NCO and 4 men
Weapons: Rifles
Options:
- Add up to 7 additional soldiers at +13pts each.
- Any soldiers may have a submachine gun instead of a rifle for +3pts each
- One soldier may have a LMG for +20pts. Another soldier becomes the loader
- The entire squad may have anti-tank grenades for +2pts per model
- Airborne squads can be *Tough Fighters* for +1pts per man
Special Rules:
- Tank hunters (if anti-tank grenades taken)
- *Tough Fighters* (if option is taken)

Russian paratroopers attack Dobrosli airstrip, by Peter Dennis © Osprey Publishing Ltd. Taken from Campaign 245: Demyansk 1942–43.

Soviet naval squad

NAVAL SQUAD

The Soviet Baltic Fleet and most of the Black Sea Fleet were bottled up in harbour by the German advance. In Leningrad, the ships of the Red Banner fleet became anti-aircraft platforms and long-range artillery for the duration of the siege. This freed up large numbers of sailors to serve as desperately needed riflemen, often still dressed in their black naval uniform with its distinctive cap and striped shirt. The Germans called them the 'black death' because of their black or dark blue uniforms. In total, about 350,000 Red Navy sailors fought on land during the Great Patriotic War. A number of specialised naval infantry units were formed: 40 brigades and five regiments. They won a reputation for tenacity and daring both in defensive fighting and in coastal landing operations on the Baltic and Black seas.

Cost: Regular Infantry 55pts or Veteran Infantry 70pts
Composition: 1 NCO and 4 men
Weapons: Rifles
Options:
- Add up to 7 additional soldiers at +11pts each (Regular) or +14pts each (Veteran)
- Any soldiers may have a submachine gun instead of a rifle for +2pts each
- Up to one soldier may have a LMG for +20pts. Another soldier becomes the loader
- The entire squad may have anti-tank grenades for +2pts per model

Special Rules:
- Tank hunters (if anti-tank grenades taken)
- *Tough Fighters*

Partisans on the move

Assault engineer squad

PARTISAN SQUAD

In the debacles of 1941 large numbers of Red Army soldiers managed to slip out of Panzer encirclements or POW camps only to find themselves trapped miles behind the German front lines. Faced with the prospect of being shot as deserters or sent to penal battalions if they returned, many of these soldiers took to the forests and marshes. Savage Nazi repression in the rear areas by SS *Einsatzgruppen* soon meant these rag-tag fighters gained popular support, which they repaid by derailing trains, looting supply dumps and ambushing rear-echelon convoys. Following his speech of 3 July 1941, Stalin ordered the Central Committee to organise the partisan movement as an extension of the Red Army by airdropping heavy weapons, supplies and personnel to bolster them. By 1942 the Germans were forced to keep 25 special security divisions, 30 regiments and more than 100 police battalions tied down in anti-partisan activities. Despite the invaders' increasingly brutal efforts, large areas of Russia effectively stayed under partisan control until liberated.

Cost: Inexperienced Infantry 35pts
Composition: 1 NCO and 4 men
Weapons: Rifles
Options:
- Add up to 7 additional soldiers with rifles at +7pts each
- The NCO may have a submachine gun instead of a rifle for +3pts
- Up to one soldier may have a LMG for +20pts. Another soldier becomes the loader
- The entire squad may have anti-tank grenades for +2pts per model
- Partisan squads can be *Shirkers* for a reduction of 3pts per man

Special Rules:
- *Shirkers* (if option is taken)
- Tank hunters (if anti-tank grenades taken)

SCOUT SQUAD

Specialised Soviet scout units were formed from 1943 onwards as the Red Army went increasingly on the offensive. The Scout units (*razvedchiki*) were forerunners of the modern *Spetznatz*

and in many ways paralleled the evolution of the British Commandos and the US Rangers. Scouts were lightly armed and equipped with camouflage coveralls. Their primary role was to find routes through or around German defences, conduct reconnaissance into rear areas and then slip back to report. Scouts would also eliminate observation posts, lay ambushes and set demolition charges to further demoralise German troops behind the front lines.

Cost: Veteran Infantry 70pts
Composition: 1 NCO and 4 men
Weapons: Rifles
Options:
- Add up to 2 additional soldiers at +14pts each
- Any soldiers may have a submachine gun instead of a rifle for +3pts each
- The entire squad may have anti-tank grenades for +2pts per model

Special Rules:
- Scouts count as Observers/Snipers for Set-Up purposes (Bolt Action rulebook page 118)
- Tank hunters (if anti-tank grenades taken)
- Behind enemy lines: When Outflanking (as described on page 119 of the Bolt Action rulebook), units of Scouts ignore the –1 modifier to the Order test for coming onto the table

ASSAULT ENGINEER SQUAD

Shortages meant that Soviet formations were sparsely served when it came to transport and rear-echelon support. Pioneer detachments were a notable exception. Their expertise was too essential to do without: bridge-building, demolitions, fortification construction and minefield placement and clearance. These all required skills the conscripted masses did not have. Assault engineers were specialists tasked with liquidating enemy strongpoints during an advance and clearing obstacles to allow tank units to breakthrough. This was extremely dangerous work with a high casualty rate (even by Red Army standards) and assault engineer units were sometimes equipped with SN-42 body armour to give them a fighting chance.

Cost: Veteran Infantry 65pts
Composition: 1 NCO and 4 men
Weapons: Rifles
Options:
- Add up to 6 additional soldiers at +13pts each
- Any soldiers may have a submachine gun instead of a rifle for +3pts each
- One soldier may have a LMG for +20pts. Another soldier becomes the loader
- One soldier can have a flamethrower instead of a rifle for +20pts. Another soldier becomes the assistant
- The entire squad may have SN-42 body armour for +5pts per model
- The entire squad may have anti-tank grenades for +2pts per model

Special Rules:
- Tank hunters (if anti-tank grenades taken)

MOTORCYCLE SQUAD

Much like the German *Kradschützen*, formations of Soviet motorcycle troops were allocated to mechanised units to serve as fast reconnaissance units roving ahead of armoured columns and seizing key objectives like bridges and road junctions. Soviet motorcycle troops rode the IMZ-Ural M-72 – a direct copy of the BMW R-71 – a sturdy beast that this author can personally attest is made out of anvils. As with cavalry the motorcycle troops were expected to use their mounts as transport to the battlefield and then dismount to fight on foot. By mid-1943 motorcycle troops were phased out and replaced with mechanised infantry in a variety of armoured carriers supplied by Lend-Lease.

Cost: Regular Infantry 50pts
Composition: 1 NCO and 4 men
Weapons: Rifles
Options:
- Add up to 6 additional men with rifles at +10pts each
- Any soldiers may have a submachine gun instead of a rifle for +3pts each
- One soldier may have a LMG for +20pts. Another soldier becomes the loader
- The entire squad may be mounted upon motorcycles and motorcycles with sidecars for +5pts per man

Special Rules:
- Tank hunters (if anti-tank grenades taken)
- Motorbikes: A mounted squad uses the motorbikes rules (see Bolt Action rulebook p71)

MEDIUM MACHINE GUN TEAM

The Red Army used the venerable Maxim Model 1910 as its medium machine gun throughout the war, the very same weapon that had served the Tsarist army in World War I. It was a capable weapon that could be tripod-, sledge- or wheel-mounted and was often given a useful shield to help preserve the crew. The Maxim was so heavy and cumbersome, however, that, unlike most other Soviet weapons, the Germans seldom made use of captured examples. The Maxim was slowly replaced by the newer, lighter but equally effective SG43 model machine gun, which was also usually deployed on a small, wheeled mount with a gun shield.

Cost: 35pts (Inexperienced), 50pts (Regular), 65pts (Veteran)
Team: 3 men – firer and 2 loaders
Weapons: 1 MMG
Options:
- Gun shield: the machine gun can have a gun shield for +5pts

Special Rules:
- Team weapon
- Fixed
- Gun shield (if fitted)

Maxim medium machine gun team

DShK HEAVY MACHINE GUN TEAM

The DShK 12.7mm belt-fed heavy machine gun was the standard Russian heavy machine gun of World War II, comparable to the US .50-cal Browning. It was used on wheeled mountings like the Maxim and could quickly be placed on a tall tripod for anti-aircraft defence. Truck-mounted and multiple versions were also employed in this role. The DShK was also seen during the late war on the cupolas of Soviet heavy tanks such as the IS-2 and ISU-152. DShK stood for its two inventors, Degtyaryov and Shpagin, and was the basis of its nickname *'Dushka'* – literally 'sweetie' or 'darling' in Russian.

Cost: 49pts (Inexperienced), 70pts (Regular), 91pts (Veteran)
Team: 4 men – firer and 3 loaders
Weapons: 1 HMG
Options:
- Gun shield: the machine gun can have a gun shield for +5pts
- Pintle-mount: the machine gun can have a pintle-mount tripod for +5pts

Special Rules:
- Team weapon
- Fixed
- Flak (if pintle-mounted)
- Gun shield (if fitted)

PTRD anti-tank rifle team

ANTI-TANK RIFLE TEAM

While the anti-tank rifle soon fell out of favour in other armies, the Soviets adopted it in 1939 after experience with Polish and Finnish models. The Soviets developed two types of their own, the bolt-action 14.5mm Degtaryev PTRD and the more sophisticated semi-automatic Simonov PTRS. A total of 202,488 PTRDs and 63,385 PTRS were built during the war and they remained in service right up to 1945. Although both types were capable of penetrating the armour of lighter German tanks, crews had to get extremely close to do so, and with the more heavily armoured German tanks their only chance was to hit through a vision port or other vulnerable spot, or else to use their guns to snipe at exposed crew members. Even so, anti-tank rifles became such a nuisance for German tank crews that, in 1943, they began up-armouring the sides and rear of their vehicles with *schürzen* skirt-plates. In the later part of the war anti-tank rifles were more often used against lighter targets such as armoured cars, half-tracks, trucks and entrenched positions.

Cost: 21pts (Inexperienced), 30pts (Regular), 39pts (Veteran)
Team: 2 men – firer and loader
Weapons: 1 Anti-tank rifle
Special Rules:
- Team weapon
- Extra selection: You may take up to 3 anti-tank teams (any mix of anti-tank rifle teams, ampulomet anti-tank teams, 'tank hunters' teams and 'dog-mines' anti-tank teams) as 1 selection in each reinforced platoon

AMPULOMET 'MOLOTOV LAUNCHER' ANTI-TANK TEAM

The Ampulomet was an unusual mortar-type weapon. Its sealed glass ampoule 'shell' was propelled by a shotgun charge and had a theoretical range of about 400 yards, but it was not very accurate. The ampoule was filled with a mixture of white phosphorus and sulphur. This shell would shatter on impact, spontaneously ignite, and burn fiercely. It was intended as an anti-tank weapon but was also used against other targets including infantry. It was not especially effective or successful and it ceased to be used from 1943.

Cost: 28pts (Inexperienced), 40pts (Regular), 52pts (Veteran)
Team: 3 men
Weapons: 1 Ampulomet
Special Rules:
- Team weapon
- Fixed
- Extra selection. You may take up to 3 anti-tank teams (any mix of anti-tank rifle teams, ampulomet anti-tank teams, 'tank hunters' teams, and 'dog-mines' anti-tank teams) as 1 selection in each reinforced platoon
- Ampulomet: this weapon has the profile below:

Type	Range	Shots	Pen	Special
Ampulomet	24"	1	HE	Team, Fixed, HE (D6)

- If an ampulomet hits an armoured vehicle and fails to penetrate its armour, roll a die. On the score of a 6 the vehicle is 'on fire' as described for a damage result of 3 on the Damage Results on Armoured Targets on page 87 of the Bolt Action rulebook.

'TANK HUNTERS' ANTI-TANK TEAM

Desperate times prompted desperate measures for the Red Army as, time and again, Panzers simply overran Soviet defences. Sometimes, the only protection available against the armoured beasts were men brave enough to crawl into forward positions and stay there until the foe came within Molotov-throwing range. As the Red Army gained equipment and experience, tank hunters were often replaced with flamethrowers or anti-tank rifles instead, though improved magnetic mines later in the war still gave Panzer crews reason to fear the tank hunters.

Cost: 20pts (Inexperienced), 28pts (Regular), 36pts (Veteran)
Team: 2 men – NCO and Private
Weapons: Rifles, anti-tank grenades
Options:
- Any soldiers may have a submachine gun instead of a rifle for +3pts each
- One soldier can have a (captured) panzerfaust in addition to other weapons for +5pts
- Add up to 2 additional men at +10pts each (Inexperienced) or +14pts each (Regular) or +18pts each (Veteran)

Special Rules:
- Tough Tank Hunters: 'Tough' tank hunters have all the usual rules for 'tank hunters' and in addition double their attacks in close combat against vehicles (i.e each soldier makes 2 attacks)
- Forward position: A tank hunter team count as Observers/Snipers for Set-Up purposes (see page 118 of the Bolt Action rulebook)
- Extra selection: You may take up to 3 anti-tank teams (any mix of anti-tank rifle teams, ampulomet anti-tank teams, 'tank hunters' teams and 'dog-mines' anti-tank teams) as 1 selection in each reinforced platoon

SOVIET INFANTRY ANTI-TANK WEAPONS

Surprisingly, despite their expertise with rocket weaponry in the form of the deadly Katyusha multiple launcher, the Soviet Union did not produce a viable infantry-portable anti-tank weapon like the American Bazooka or German panzerfaust. A great reliance was placed on lightweight, conventional anti-tank guns, and even outmoded anti-tank rifles, to fight off German tanks and armoured carriers. Many improvised solutions were tried, most famously the widespread use of 'Molotov cocktails' – bottles of petrol or kerosene ignited by a flaming rag stuck in the top. These were used in such numbers that some Soviet factories mass-produced special 'KS bottles' which performed the same purpose, using a small packet of chemicals as a (moderately) safer method of ignition.

A more curious weapon was the *ampulomet*, a basic mortar that fired a spherical vial containing napalm at ranges up to 250m. It was both inaccurate and not very effective when it hit, so it soon fell out of use after 1941. Perhaps most desperate of all was the use of specially trained 'anti-tank mine dogs'. The dogs were outfitted with two panniers containing explosives, and a trigger lever protruding above their shoulders. Training consisted of repeatedly feeding the dogs underneath tanks until such a time as the unfortunate (and, presumably at this point, hungry) animals were released onto the battlefield to hopefully seek their dinner beneath a Panzer. Russian accounts claim as many as 300 German tanks were destroyed in this way. The Germans dispute the effectiveness of the mine-dogs and maintain the only real effect was to encourage them to shoot all stray dogs on sight.

8,500 bazookas were supplied to the Soviets under Lend-Lease, but this small number seems to have disappeared into the millions-strong warfront virtually without trace. Red Army soldiers developed a lot of respect for the disposable panzerfaust launchers when they appeared, and would use captured ones whenever they had the opportunity. Ultimately, one of the best infantry anti-tank weapons in the Red Army's arsenal proved to be the RPG-43 – an awkward, hand thrown (the 'R' is for *ruchnaya* – 'hand-held' in Russian, not 'rocket') shaped charge grenade introduced in 1943. More effective still were conventional mines buried at night by Soviet sappers along likely approach routes for armour. At the battle of Kursk special 'mobile obstacle detachments' were formed for this very purpose.

DOG MINES ANTI-TANK TEAM

Before the war the Soviets had experimented with using dogs to deliver explosives to different kinds of enemy target. The original idea was for the dog to drop its charge and return to its handler, but this proved ineffective – many dogs dutifully brought the deadly explosive back to their handlers with disastrous results for all concerned. A less complex solution was to fit the dogs with a mechanism – a simple lever – that would trigger the charge as soon as a dog dived beneath an enemy tank or vehicle, hopefully destroying the tank along with the dog. Although dog mines were used in action, their effectiveness is not easy to assess. Many dogs simply ran from the noise and smells of battle whilst others bolted for the safety of Soviet machines or trenches. The Germans where sufficiently startled to shoot all dogs on sight. Dog mines gradually fell out of use after 1942. They are credited with destroying a number of German tanks at the battle of Kursk. In Bolt Action we consider the dog to be a one-shot weapon that can be 'fired' (i.e. released) by its handler against a vehicle target within range.

Cost: 26pts (Inexperienced), 36pts (Regular), 46pts (Veteran)
Team: 2 handlers – NCO and Private
Weapons: Each handler has a rifle, anti-tank grenades and a dog mine
Options:
- Any handler may have a submachine gun instead of a rifle for +3pts each
- Add up to 2 additional handlers (equipped as above) at +13pts each (Inexperienced) or +18pts each (Regular) or +23pts each (Veteran)

Special Rules:
- Tank hunters
- Extra selection: You may take up to 3 anti-tank teams (any mix of anti-tank rifle teams, ampulomet anti-tank teams, 'tank hunters' teams and 'dog-mines' anti-tank teams) as 1 selection in each reinforced platoon
- Dog mines: A dog mine is a one-shot weapon with a range of 18". Dog mines can only target stationary vehicles (i.e. any vehicle that is not sporting an order dice showing a Run or Advance order). Dog mines are fired as normal, except that instead of rolling to hit, roll on the following chart. Note that if a Recce vehicle reacts to the dog mine attack by moving, the dog mine automatically scores a 2-3. :

Result	Effect
1	The dog, due to familiarity with Soviet vehicles, hits the closest friendly stationary vehicle within range instead of the target (no line of sight is needed in this case). Resolve the hit as described for 4–6 below. If no target presents itself see 2–3 below
2–3	The dog is either gunned down or bolts from the noise of battle and deserts, possibly lured by the smell of German sausages. The traitor will be shot on sight by political officers
4–6	The dog scampers to the target, crawls underneath and explodes. The vehicle suffers a hit with a Pen of +5 (no Pen modifiers apply)

A Red Army marksman picks out his next target

SNIPER TEAM

The sniper became synonymous with the Red Army, particularly during the grim sieges of Stalingrad and Leningrad. 'Sniper schools' were established in bombed-out buildings and cellars, where successful snipers passed down their skills to ever-growing numbers of students – many of them women. Soviet propaganda lavished attention on successful snipers and encouraged a doctrine of 'sniperism' among the troops. Snipers used telescopic sights on either a bolt action Moisin–Nagant 1891/30 or, more rarely, a Tokarev SVT-40 semi automatic rifle. A variety of ammunition was used, including tracer and armour-piercing rounds. Soviet snipers were available at company level working as teams or sometimes on their own. Individual Red Army squads would often have a designated marksman with a scoped rifle to help compensate for the lack of long-range firepower due to the large numbers of submachine guns in use. Soviet snipers became renowned for their fieldcraft, stealth and patience. The most successful snipers each accounted for hundreds of enemy – around 500 being the greatest tally recorded by a single sniper.

Cost: 50pts (Regular), 65pts (Veteran)
Team: 2 – sniper and assistant
Weapons: 1 Rifle
Special Rules:
- Team weapon
- Sniper

FLAMETHROWER TEAM

The Soviets made great use of flamethrowers including FOG-1 static types dug in to cover bunkers and trenches. Due to

shortcomings in developing other credible anti-tank weapons, Red Army doctrine placed strong emphasis on using flamethrowers as anti-tank as well as anti-infantry weapons. They even formed separate motorised anti-tank flamethrower battalions in 1943. By far the most common Russian flamethrowers were the man-packed ROKS types. The ROKS-2 was designed with a fuel tank that looked like an ordinary backpack and a nozzle resembling a rifle, so as not to attract unwelcome attention on the battlefield.

Cost: 50pts (Regular), 65pts (Veteran)
Team: 2 – flamethrower and assistant
Weapons: 1 Infantry flamethrower
Options:
- Make flamethrower ROKS-2 for +5pts
Special Rules:
- Flamethrower
- Team weapon
- ROKS-2: If this option is chosen then the flamethrower armed man cannot be chosen as an 'exceptional damage' result. The flamethrower operator is indistinguishable from an ordinary rifleman.

LIGHT MORTAR TEAM

The standard light mortar used by Russian infantry during World War II was the 50mm Infantry Mortar Model 1940 (50-PM 40), a cheaper version of the earlier Model 1938. In addition, the Soviet army received considerable numbers of 2-inch mortars from Britain via Lend-Lease. The 50mm was deemed a 'company' mortar as opposed to the heavier 82mm battalion and 120mm

A medium mortar team prepares to rain destruction on the Fascist invaders

regimental mortars. The allocation of 50mm mortars was initially to individual teams at platoon level, but later they were more often concentrated together at company level for use en masse. The weapon was easily man-portable and could lay down high explosive or smoke bombs at a range of over 800 yards.

Cost: 24pts (Inexperienced), 35pts (Regular), 46pts (Veteran)
Team: 2 – firer and loader.
Weapons: 1 Light mortar
Special Rules:
- Team weapon
- Indirect fire
- HE (D3)

MEDIUM MORTAR TEAM
The standard Russian medium mortar of the war was the 82-PM-41 or 82mm battalion mortar Model 1941. This served alongside the otherwise similar 82mm Model 1937. Both were very effective and accurate weapons with a range of about 3,000 yards. 82mm mortars were regarded as artillery rather than infantry weapons by the Russians and were usually massed together in batteries for battalion-level support.

Cost: 35pts (Inexperienced), 50pts (Regular), 65pts (Veteran)
Team: 3 – firer and 2 loaders
Weapons: 1 Medium mortar
Options:
- May add Spotter for +10 points
Special Rules:
- Team weapon
- Fixed
- Indirect fire
- HE (D6)

120mm heavy mortar team

HEAVY MORTAR TEAM
The Red Army pioneered the modern heavy mortar and Germans feared them greatly, so much so that they copied the Russian 120mm weapon almost identically and used them themselves with great effect. The 120mm mortar had a range of about 6,000 yards. Although even heavier mortars were produced, these were breech-loading weapons with carriages that required towing vehicles to move, making them true artillery pieces.

Cost: 46pts (Inexperienced), 65pts (Regular), 84pts (Veteran)
Team: 4 – firer and 3 loaders
Weapons: 1 Heavy mortar
Options:
- May add Spotter for +10 points
Special Rules:
- Team weapon
- Fixed
- Indirect fire
- HE (2D6)

ARTILLERY

FIELD ARTILLERY

In Russia artillery is referred to as the 'God of War' (*Bog Vynoy*) and has formed the senior arm of the military since before the time of Napoleon. The Soviet army deployed artillery in vast numbers and a bewildering variety of sizes, from light infantry guns to huge divisional artillery pieces. During the Great Patriotic War the Central Committee held back large numbers of artillery pieces from regimental and divisional organisation levels in order to mass them into separate artillery regiments, brigades, divisions and even corps for maximum effect. German accounts of the Eastern Front always emphasise the ubiquity of Red Army artillery and weight of Soviet barrages.

LIGHT HOWITZER

The Russians produced a number of different light artillery guns of the same 76.2mm (3-inch) caliber. The following entry is suitable for the old Tsarist Model 1927/39 regimental gun and its variants and 76.2mm ZiS-3 divisional guns without access to armour-piercing ammunition – something that would be a criminal oversight after 1942. By the late war the ZiS-3 divisional gun had become the Red Army's chief field gun – a good all round weapon that Stalin called 'a masterpiece of artillery design'. The ZiS-3 was used both as a howitzer and against enemy tanks to such good effect that we have included it in the Bolt Action game as an anti-tank gun, though with the ability to operate as a light howitzer (see page 40).

Cost: 40pts (Inexperienced), 50pts (Regular), 60pts (Veteran)
Team: 3 – firer and 2 loaders.
Weapons: 1 Light howitzer

Special Rules:
- Gun shield
- Team weapon
- Fixed
- Howitzer
- HE (D6)

MEDIUM HOWITZER

Red Army medium artillery consisted of 122mm artillery pieces together with a few older 107mm guns (most of which were lost in the 1941 fighting). The 122mm A19 gun was a robust, successful design that was later developed into the D-25S for self-propelled guns and the D-25T for the IS-2 heavy tank. Although the A19 was too slow-firing and cumbersome to make an effective anti-tank gun, it was certainly capable of destroying heavy German tanks. By 1943, the heaviest German Panzers were practically invulnerable to smaller weapons, and the 122mm A19 was one of the few effective answers the Red Army had to them.

Cost: 60pts (Inexperienced), 75pts (Regular), 90pts (Veteran)
Team: 4 – firer and 3 loaders
Weapons: 1 Medium howitzer
Options:
- May add Spotter for +10 points
Special Rules:
- Gun shield
- Team weapon
- Fixed
- Howitzer
- HE (2D6)

ARTILLERY – THE RUSSIAN GOD OF WAR

Heavy artillery barrages, especially at the opening of an offensive, became one of the Red Army's calling cards. One of the main tactical insights of the German's Eastern Front 'defensive expert' Colonel-General Heinrici was to withdraw his men from their forward positions when he had had determined a Soviet attack was imminent. Some insight can be gained into the kind of terror experienced by those on the front lines by describing the opening barrages of Operation *Bagration* at 0500hrs on the 23 June 1944.

Battery density for the operation was extremely high with over 24,000 artillery pieces concentrated on four sections of the front with approximately two tons of ammunition for each weapon (roughly 160 rounds for a 122mm howitzer). Fire plans varied, but on average the opening barrage lasted for two hours. Most featured an initial 10–20-minute intensive surprise barrage against the forward German trenches up to a depth of 6 kilometres, with the aim of crushing the trench lines and catching exposed troops before they could withdraw deeper into the defences. Each artillery piece fired at an increasing rate, so that by the last five minutes of the initial barrage every piece was firing as fast as possible.

This was followed by a rolling barrage, or a double rolling barrage in areas where defences were particularly dense. Massed Katyusha rocket launchers fired every five to seven minutes during the barrage to completely saturate areas already being pounded by conventional artillery. German attempts at counter-battery fire were engaged with specialist long-range artillery and crushed. German accounts of the opening barrage of Operation *Bagration* universally described it as being of an intensity and destructiveness never before seen during the war.

HEAVY HOWITZER

The 152mm ML-20 gun-howitzer was the main heavy gun used by the Soviet army. It was augmented by older M10 howitzers and, towards the end of the war, by the new D1 152mm howitzer. This latter gun was a much more mobile weapon that would go on to serve in Soviet and post-Soviet armies to this day. All were capable, long-ranged weapons that would typically be deployed well behind the fighting zone – having a range of more than 7 miles. This category includes the MT-13 160mm breech-loading mortar introduced in 1944 and is also suitable for the 203mm B-4 Howitzer Model 1931, the 152mm BR-2 gun Model 1935 and the 280mm BR-5 Mortar Model 1939 with their common tracked carriages.

Cost: 92pts (Inexperienced), 115pts (Regular), 138pts (Veteran)
Team: 5 – firer and 4 loaders
Weapons: 1 Heavy howitzer
Options:
- May add Spotter for +10 points

Special Rules:
- Gun shield
- Team weapon
- Fixed
- Howitzer (replaced with Indirect Fire, if the weapon is a mortar)
- HE (3D6)

ANTI-AIRCRAFT GUNS

Soviet air defence was the responsibility of the PVO (*Voyska ProtivoVozdushnoy Oborony*, literally 'Anti-Air Defence Troops') at a national level. Most anti-aircraft weapons were allocated to the PVO while Red Army organic air defence was often thin on the ground, particularly at battalion and regimental levels. The Red Army used two main types of towed anti-aircraft weapon in 25mm and 37mm calibres.

37MM 61-K MODEL 1939

After experimentation with a number of different weapons in the 1930s the Red Army purchased several 40mm Bofors automatic anti-aircraft guns from Sweden. The 37mm 61-K Model 1939 was heavily influenced by the Bofors design and became the most common divisional anti-aircraft weapon during the Great Patriotic War. Some 20,000 were produced by 1945.

Cost: 48pts (Inexperienced), 60pts (Regular), 72pts (Veteran)
Team: 4 – gunner and 3 loaders
Weapons: 1 Heavy automatic cannon

Special Rules:
- Team weapon
- Fixed
- Flak

25MM72-K MODEL 1940

Much like the larger 37mm 61-K Model 1939, the 25mm 72-K Model 1940 was based on Bofors anti-aircraft guns purchased from Sweden. It was a weapon intended for the PVO, but a few found their way into the Red Army when 37mm cannon were unavailable.

Cost: 40pts (Inexperienced), 50pts (Regular), 60pts (Veteran)
Team: 3 – gunner and 2 loaders
Weapons: 1 Light automatic cannon
Special Rules:
- Team weapon
- Fixed
- Gun shield
- Flak

ANTI-TANK GUNS

At the beginning of the Great Patriotic War the Red Army primarily fielded one variety of anti-tank gun – the 45mm Model 1937. The 45mm anti-tank gun was to remain in service until the end of the war, but had to be successively supplemented by larger and more effective weapons as tank armour increased. More effective by far was the ZiS-2 57mm anti-tank gun, which became the standard weapon of anti-tank artillery regiments in mid-1943, and which was also used by the anti-tank platoons of some infantry regiments. Soviet divisional artillery was often called upon to fight tanks and issued with armour-piercing ammunition that was identical to that used for tank guns. Later in the war, shells were designed based on captured German ammunition and issued to lower velocity weapons such as the 76mm regimental guns and 122mm howitzers.

45MM MODEL 1937 ANTI-TANK GUN

The 45mm Model 1937 was derived from the German Rheinmetall 37mm PaK 36. The PaK 36 was produced under license in the Soviet Union from 1931 as the 37mm anti-tank gun Model 1930. Soviet designers considered the 37mm underpowered and mounted a heavier gun tube on the existing 37mm carriage and modified it to fire standard 45mm tank gun ammunition. The resulting weapon was light, versatile and a powerful anti-tank weapon for its day. Soviet industry produced 37,354 45mm Model 1937 anti-tank guns before switching over to the improved M-42 model in 1943.

Take aim, comrade! A 45mm anti-tank gun and Komsomolets tractor lie in wait for the enemy

Cost: 40pts (Inexperienced), 50pts (Regular), 60pts (Veteran)
Weapons: 1 Light anti-tank gun
Team: 2
Special Rules:
- Gun shield
- Team weapon
- Fixed

M-42 ANTI-TANK GUN

The 1937 model 45mm anti-tank gun was a relatively effective weapon at the outset of Barbarossa, but by 1942 it stood no chance against heavily armoured German tanks like the Tiger. Modifications were made to increase the barrel length of the 45mm to improve its velocity and penetration. 'Sub-calibre' (HVAP/APCR) ammunition was also developed but the improved 45mm was still unable to achieve frontal penetrations against the new German heavy tanks at anything other than point-blank range. However, it was still a useful weapon easily capable of destroying light vehicles, and it remained in service in very large numbers (some 10,843 were manufactured). In the late war the 45mm was more often used as an infantry gun firing high explosives than as an anti-tank weapon.

Cost: 46pts (Inexperienced), 58pts (Regular), 70pts (Veteran)
Weapons: 1 Light anti-tank gun
Team: 2
Special Rules:
- Gun shield
- Team weapon
- Fixed
- Improved ballistics: At short range an M-42 anti-tank gun adds +1 to its penetration value

ZIS-2 ANTI-TANK GUN

The 57mm ZiS-2 was developed before the war to give anti-tank artillery regiments a weapon capable of detroying heavily armoured tanks. It was a rapid-firing semi-automatic gun that could shoot up to 25 rounds a minute. ZiS-2 production was cancelled shortly after the outbreak of war when it became clear that the armour thickness of German tanks had been greatly exaggerated. Instead anti-tank units persisted with the old 45mm M-42 and 76.2mm ZiS-3 divisional gun. However, by late 1942 these weapons were no longer capable of facing the new tanks deployed by the Germans, and production of the ZiS-2 was given the full go ahead in June 1943. Almost 10,000 were made before the war ended.

Cost: 60pts (Inexperienced), 75pts (Regular), 90pts (Veteran)
Team: 3
Weapon: 1 Medium anti-tank gun
Special Rules:
- Gun shield
- Team weapon
- Fixed

ZIS-3 DIVISIONAL GUN

The ZiS-3 was a truly multi-purpose weapon that was used as artillery and as an anti-tank gun by the Red Army. The Germans came to know it well and dubbed it the '*Ratsch-Baum*' ('crash-boom') for its distinctive sound. By the battle of Kursk in 1943, ZiS-3 batteries were routinely dug in to fire initially as howitzers and then switch to an anti-tank role to stop breakthroughs. Ironically, as a stopgap the Germans also used captured Russian 76.2mm guns as anti-tank weapons until the arrival of the 75mm PaK 40. Close to 70,000 76.2mm field guns

ZiS-3 divisional gun

were produced by the Soviets during the Great Patriotic War and the vast majority of them were ZiS-3s. In the Bolt Action game we count the ZiS-3 as both an anti-tank gun and a howitzer to reflect its remarkable versatility.

Cost: 54pts (Inexperienced), 80pts (Regular), 96pts (Veteran)
Team: 4
Weapons: 1 Medium anti-tank gun and light howitzer
Special Rules:
- Gun shield
- Team weapon
- Fixed
- Versatile: The ZiS-3 Can also fire as a light howitzer

85MM MODEL 1939

The 85mm Model 1939 was an anti-aircraft weapon intended for high- to medium-altitude air defence that saw some limited frontline service. Unlike the Germans, the Red Army seldom used its AA guns for anti-tank work, possibly due to their relative scarcity. In 1943, however, several anti-tank brigades equipped with 85mm guns were formed in response to the emergence of new German heavy tank designs. This was undertaken as a temporary measure until heavier anti-tank guns and tank destroyers became available. The 85mm Model 1939 was subsequently developed into the successful D5-T and ZiS-53 tank guns used on the SU-85 and T34-85.

Cost: 88pts (Inexperienced), 110pts (Regular), 132pts (Veteran)
Team: 4
Weapons: 1 Heavy anti-tank gun
Options:
- Gun shield: the gun can have a gun shield for +5pts
Special Rules:
- Team weapon
- Fixed
- Flak
- Gun Shield (if fitted)

A-19 FIELD GUN

The A-19 122mm field gun was less than ideal as an anti-tank weapon due to its size, slow traverse and rate of fire. However the Red Army was nothing if not adaptive to necessity, and the weapon was pressed into service against German Tigers, Panthers and Elefants. As was found with the later 122mm-armed IS-2 heavy tank, the shells had too low a velocity to have great penetrating power, but their sheer size and weight still inflicted catastrophic damage on whatever they hit. As with the ZiS-3 divisional gun, we treat the A-19 field gun as both an anti-tank gun and a howitzer to reflect its remarkable versatility.

Cost: 80pts (Inexperienced), 100pts (Regular), 120pts (Veteran)
Team: 4
Weapons: 1 Heavy anti-tank gun and medium howitzer
Special Rules:
- Gun shield
- Team weapon
- Fixed
- Versatile: The A-19 can also fire as a medium howitzer
- Less than ideal: When firing as an anti-tank gun the A-19 always receives the -1 to hit modifier as if it were firing at long range, and it never receives the +1 modifier for firing at pointblank range

BS-3 ANTI-TANK GUN

The model 1944 BS-3 100mm gun was a development of a naval anti-aircraft gun, used primarily as an anti-tank weapon. Although it could serve as a field gun, its smaller shell made it less effective in this role than the 122mm A-19 howitzer. The BS-3 equipped light artillery brigades within tank armies along with the ubiquitous ZiS-3 field gun. About 600 were produced before the war ended, of which 185 were in service by January 1945.

Cost: 88pts (Inexperienced), 110pts (Regular), 132pts (Veteran)
Team: 5
Weapons: 1 Heavy anti-tank gun
Special Rules:
- Gun shield
- Team weapon
- Fixed

VEHICLES

TANKS

In 1940 the Soviets were reckoned to have the largest number of tanks in the world – 23,106 all told, more than all the other combatant nations combined. By the end of 1941, over 90% of this gigantic horde had been captured or destroyed by the Axis invaders. Enormous numbers were lost to mechanical breakdown and air attack before they even reached the front lines. Once in battle, inexperienced Red Army tankers were torn apart by the veteran Panzer forces. As with all aspects of the Great Patriotic War, the Red Army stolidly absorbed staggering losses and fought on – often without tank support for much of 1942. Once Soviet factories were re-established in the east, Russian tanks were produced in vast quantities – 76,827 tanks of all classes were manufactured between 1941 and 1945. The tank produced in greater numbers than any other was the iconic T-34 – arguably the best all-round medium tank of the war. The Russians also used many Lend-Lease vehicles, including British and American tanks. These proved inferior to the Russian's own designs and by the late war most of these had gone, apart from significant numbers of M4A2 Sherman tanks.

T-26 LIGHT TANK

The T-26 was based on the 1928 British Vickers '6-ton' light tank design. It served with some distinction in the Spanish Civil War, although the Red Army drew erroneous conclusions about massed armour formations based on their experiences there. Over 10,000 T-26s were in service at the opening of *Barbarossa*, including specialist command vehicles and flamethrower tanks. They were mainly operated in independent light tank brigades or in tank battalions assigned to support Rifle divisions. Ninety percent of T-26s broke down or were destroyed in the fighting within the first few weeks. A few T-26s soldiered on past the initial cull in odd corners, some serving in besieged Leningrad right up to 1944 and a few even participating in the Soviet defeat of the Japanese in Manchuria in 1945. The T-26's armour was very light by 1940's standards so we shall rate it as equivalent to an armoured carrier.

T-26A LIGHT TANK

Principal service: 1931–41. Numbers manufactured: 2,038.

Cost: 56pts (Inexperienced), 70pts (Regular), 84pts (Veteran)
Weapons: 2 (separate) turret-mounted MMGs
Damage Value: 7+ (Armoured Carrier)

T-26B LIGHT TANK

Principal service: 1931–41. Numbers manufactured: 4,192 plus 3,887 with radios.
Cost: 84pts (Inexperienced), 105pts (Regular), 126pts (Veteran)
Weapons: 1 turret-mounted light anti-tank gun with co-axial MMG
Damage Value: 7+ (Armoured Carrier)

OT-26 AND OT-133 LIGHT FLAMETHROWER TANK

Principal service: 1933–41. Numbers manufactured: Approximately 1,200.
Cost: 84pts (Inexperienced), 105pts (Regular), 126pts (Veteran)
Weapons: 1 turret-mounted flamethrower with co-axial MMG
Damage Value: 7+ (Armoured Carrier)

Special Rules:
- Internal, volatile fuel tanks makes each tank a potential fireball. Flame-throwing vehicles are more likely to be destroyed by damage, as explained on page 52 of the rulebook.

BT-5 AND BT-7 LIGHT TANK

BT stood for *Bystrokhodny tank* – 'fast/high speed tank' and were a design of Soviet cavalry tanks that emphasised light weight and high speed. They were based on designs by American J. Walter Christie that featured hard rubber road wheels and a chain drive that allowed them to run without tracks. While impressively fast at 53mph for the BT-7, the BT series were lightly armoured and their gasoline engines made them fire-prone. The BT tanks were already scheduled for replacement by the T-34 in 1940, all production had halted before the invasion began and the existing formations still using them were decimated in the summer fighting. Surviving BT tanks were withdrawn from the front after mid-1942 and seem to have vanished into training and far eastern commands. Although the BT-7 was both larger and heavier than the BT-5, the practical differences between them are marginal enough that both are treated as having the same characteristics in Bolt Action terms. Principal service: 1932–41. Numbers manufactured: 7,000–8,000.

Cost: 100pts (Inexperienced), 125pts (Regular), 150pts (Veteran)
Weapons: 1 turret-mounted light anti-tank gun with co-axial MMG
Damage Value: 8+ (Light Tank)
Options:
- A BT-7A may replace its light anti-tank gun with a light howitzer for free

Five Soviet T-60s capture Tiger 100, 18 January 1943, by Peter Dennis © Osprey Publishing Ltd.
Taken from Campaign 215: Leningrad 1941–44.

T-37 LIGHT TANK

In the early 1930s, the Red Army started to look for an improved version of their earlier T-27 light tankette which had never performed satisfactorily. The subsequent design of the T-37 was heavily influenced by the contemporary Carden-Loyd tankette and the Vickers floating tank, but also reused the designs of several components from the earlier T-27. Problems were encountered in mass-producing the buoyant hull for the T-37 and this led to few (in Soviet terms) being manufactured at first. The T-37 saw action in the Winter War against Finland and the Soviet invasion of Poland before most examples of the type were destroyed in the opening weeks of the Great Patriotic War. Allegedly, a few T-37s survived in frontline service as late as 1944, presumably in the northern sectors where their amphibious capabilities would go some way to compensate for their thin armour and weak armament. Principal service: 1935–44. Numbers manufactured: Approximately 1,200.

Cost: 52pts (Inexperienced), 65pts (Regular), 78pts (Veteran)

Weapons: 1 turret-mounted MMG
Damage Value: 7+ (Armoured Carrier)
Special Rules:
- A T-37 is amphibious and can move through otherwise impassable water as explained on page 97 of the rulebook

T-40 LIGHT TANK

The tiny T-40 was introduced to replace earlier amphibious tankettes as a scouting and reconnaissance vehicle. It had a boat-shaped hull and a propeller for motive power in the water, and was armed with a DShK heavy machine gun plus a co-axial DT machine gun for self defence. Only a few hundred T-40 had been built when war broke out, and manufacture of amphibious vehicles soon took second place to replacing the horrific losses mounting daily. The T-60 light tank had already been developed from the T-40 chassis and existing manufacturing was turned over to produce this (marginally) more useful vehicle. The last batch of T-40s were completed with BM-8-24 rocket rails instead of turrets. Principal service: 1938–42. Numbers manufactured: 222.

ROYAL TIGERS

On the evening of 11 August 1944, Lt Aleksandr P. Oskin of the 53rd Guards Tank Brigade (part of the 6th Guards Tank Corps) was on patrol at the Polish village of Ogledow where he had been ordered to link up with the brigade's adjacent 2nd battalion. Unknown to him, he was about to participate in the Red Army's first encounter of the war with Germany's new wonder weapon – the Panzerkampfwagen Tiger Ausf B – a tank that was to become known to the allies as the Royal or King Tiger. The King Tiger featured well-sloped armour like that of the Panther, combined with a 8.8cm KwK 43 L/71 main gun – a potent weapon capable of defeating any Allied tank in currently in service at ranges up to 2.5km.

Arriving at the village, Lt Oskin found no sign of the 2nd battalion, but observed an approaching German column. On reporting the sighting to his brigade commander, Oskin was ordered to take a defensive position and observe the enemy. With the aid of his tank rider infantry (an experienced squad that had served with Oskin's tanks since June) he concealed the T-34/85s of his patrol in a cornfield outside the village and waited. The Germans entered the village and shot it up before halting there overnight. The next morning a column of three King Tigers moved out of the village along the road to make an attack on the Soviet bridgehead over the Vistula River at Sandomierz.

Oskin's opponents were a platoon of the sPzAbt 501, a heavy tank battalion that had disembarked at Kielche on 11 August with 45 King Tigers. However, the 45km road march from Kielche to Ogledow had reduced the battalion to just eight (some sources say eleven) operational tanks mainly due to mechanical failures in the King Tiger's criminally overstressed power plants. The 70-ton King Tigers seem to have particularly struggled with the sandy ground in the area.

Still unnoticed by the King Tigers as they left the village, Oskin waited

patiently until they were flank-on to his position at 200 meters' range before slamming a round into the turret of the middle heavy tank. Despite using a precious BR-365P hypervelocity round, the hit had no visible effect. The shot in fact penetrated and caused several casualties inside the King Tiger, but this was unknown to the Soviet tankers at the time. Oskin ordered his gunner to hit the turret of the King Tiger twice more before giving up and shooting at the rear hull to ignite the fuel tank. The King Tiger finally began to burn.

Meanwhile the lead King Tiger was swinging around its turret to find their attackers, but the dust raised by Oskin's 85mm hits temporarily blinded it. Oskin's tank hit the King Tiger three times on its turret front and bounced off each time. The fourth hit, however, penetrated turret ring and started an ammunition fire that blew off its turret. The third King Tiger had also been blinded by the smoke produced by the burning middle tank and began to quickly back off. Seeing this, Oskin triggered the MDSh smoke cans attached to the rear of his own tank for some cover and set off in pursuit. The quicker T-34/85 soon caught up with the lumbering heavy tank and knocked it out with a shot from the rear into its engine compartment. Oskin's tank riders took some of the surviving crew from the King Tiger platoon as prisoners, and the third King Tiger knocked out was later recovered and sent to the Red Army proving ground at Kubinka for testing – where it remains to this day.

The rest of sPzAbt 501 were to have little better luck, as they were caught in further ambushes by T-34/85s, IS-122s and IS-2s around Sandomierz, losing as many as 14 in total. Ultimately, while it was a superb defensive tank, the King Tiger proved too slow and underpowered to be effective in an attacking role. Lt Oskin was awarded the Hero of the Soviet Union Gold Star for actions in defeating the first Eastern Front outing of the Royal Tigers.

Cost: 64pts (Inexperienced), 80pts (Regular), 96pts (Veteran)
Weapons: 1 turret-mounted HMG with co-axial MMG
Damage Value: 7+ (Armoured Carrier)
Special Rules:
- A T-40 is amphibious and can move through otherwise impassable water as explained on page 97 of the rulebook

T-50 LIGHT INFANTRY TANK

The T-50 tank was an effort to produce a light infantry support tank – an oxymoron if ever there was one. The design was surprisingly advanced, however, with well-sloped armour and a three-man turret – an advance that would be sorely missed by overworked T-34 commanders. However, the T-34 could do everything the T-50 could do, but better, and was cheaper to build. The T-50 design was discontinued after just 69 were built, although these did see action at Leningrad, one being captured and used by the Finnish. As even these small numbers qualify as an entire class of vehicles in some World War II armies, the T-50 is presented here out of completeness. Principal service: 1939–42. Numbers manufactured: 69.

Cost: 100pts (Inexperienced), 125pts (Regular), 150pts (Veteran)
Weapons: 1 turret-mounted light anti-tank gun with co-axial MMG
Damage Value: 8+ (Light Tank)

T-60 LIGHT TANK

The T-60 was designed using the T-40 amphibious chassis with additional armour and a heavier weapon in an effort to create a more viable scout tank. The T-60's main armament was a 20mm cannon developed from the ShVAK aircraft weapon and it proved inadequate against German armour in combat. Efforts to upgrade the T-60's turret armament were unsuccessful and the T-70 was developed in its place. T-60 tanks were often converted into ammunition carriers and prime movers, and along with the T-70, formed the principal chassis for the later SU-76 self-propelled gun. Principal service: 1941–45. Numbers manufactured: 6,292.

Cost: 94pts (Inexperienced), 105pts (Regular), 116pts (Veteran)
Weapons: 1 turret-mounted light automatic cannon with co-axial MMG
Damage Value: 8+ (Light Tank)

T-70 LIGHT TANK

By the mid-war the Russians had ceased production of light tanks and turned over most of their manufacturing capability to more effective self-propelled guns and prime movers. The T-70 was the last light tank produced in any numbers and it remained in service throughout the war even after production terminated in October 1943. The T-70 was armed with a 45mm anti-tank gun and co-axial machine gun. Principal service: 1942–45. Numbers manufactured: 8,226.

T-34/76 obr.1942 medium tank

Cost: 100pts (Inexperienced), 125pts (Regular), 150pts (Veteran)
Weapons: 1 turret-mounted light anti-tank gun with co-axial MMG
Damage Value: 8+ (Light Tank)

T-28 MEDIUM TANK

The design of the T-28 was heavily influenced by the 1926-vintage Vickers A1E1 Independent tank and in 1933 it was one of the first true medium tanks to enter series production anywhere in the world. It featured some advanced features for its time, such as an anti-aircraft machine gun and a radio fitted as standard. However the T-28's armour protection and suspension were sub-par while its multi-turreted layout made it vulnerable to damage. Many of the T-28s in service in 1941 were lost to mechanical breakdown and the remainder fared poorly in combat with more modern Panzers. It vanished entirely from the frontlines by the end of the year. Due to its thin skin and poor design, we rate the T-28 as having armour equal to a light tank. Principal service: 1933–41. Numbers manufactured: 503.

Cost: 124pts (Inexperienced), 155pts (Regular), 186pts (Veteran)
Weapons: 1 turret-mounted light howitzer with co-axial MMG,
   1 turret-mounted MMG covering the front and left arcs,
   1 turret-mounted MMG covering the front and right arcs,
   1 pintle-mounted AA MMG.
Damage Value: 8+ (Light Tank)
Options:
- T-28C: Applique armour was added to the T-28c in 1940, increasing frontal armour thickness to 80mm. To represent a T-28c, add +1 damage value to the front facing and reduce the tank's speed to *Slow* for +10pts

T-34 MEDIUM TANK

Originally designed as a cavalry tank to replace the BT series, the T-34 proved to be a truly revolutionary design. Fast, extremely well armed and armoured for its time, the T-34s already in service gave the Germans a nasty shock when they invaded. The T-34 was produced in greater numbers than any other tank of the war, with production exceeding 1,200 *per month* from 1942 onwards. Although major redesigns that would impact on production were forbidden, the T-34 was continually upgraded with better armour and improved guns, making it a match for the German Panzer IV and a worthy opponent of Panthers, Tigers and heavier German tanks. By 1944, the earlier production version armed with the 76.2mm F-34 gun had been replaced by the T-34/85 armed with an 85mm ZiS-S-53 gun in a larger, three-man turret. However, the earlier tank continued in production, both fighting until the end of the war and – in the case of the T-34/85 – well beyond. The flamethrower variant of the T-34 was produced in 1942 – the OT-34, which replaced the hull machine gun with an ATO-41 (later ATO-42) flamethrower. Principal service: 1940–45. Numbers manufactured: 34,091 (some sources say 34,780), 1,170 as OT-34.

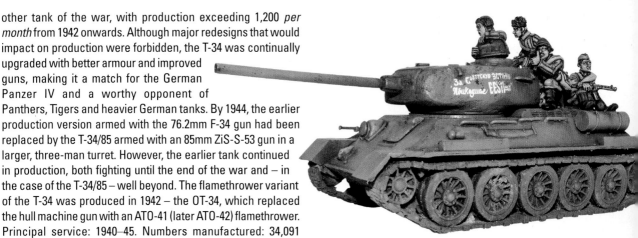

T-34/85 and tank riders

Cost: 156pts (Inexperienced), 195pts (Regular), 234pts (Veteran)
Weapons: 1 turret-mounted medium anti-tank gun with co-axial MMG and forward-facing hull-mounted MMG
Damage Value: 9+ (Medium Tank)
Options:
- OT-34: Replace hull-mounted MMG with flamethrower for +40pts. Flame-throwing vehicles are more likely to be destroyed by damage, as explained on page 52 of the Bolt Action rulebook

T-34/85 MEDIUM TANK

In 1941, the design for the T-34 was virtually frozen except for minor improvements that would ease production. By the battle of Kursk in 1943, it was apparent that the new generation of German tanks were getting too heavily armed and armoured for the T-34 to handle. The T-34/85 was created to regain parity by mating an 85mm gun turret developed for the T-44 and KV-85 onto a T-34 hull with a widened turret ring. The T-34/85 was the ultimate version of the T-34 tank. The larger turret was big enough to accommodate a third crewman, so the commander no longer had to also act as the tank's gunner, which greatly improved combat effectiveness. The 85mm ZiS-S-53 gun gave more fighting power to the T-34, which had found itself increasingly out-shot by later German tanks. A flamethrower variant of the T-34/85 was also produced, the OT-34/85, in limited numbers. Principal service: 1943–45. Numbers manufactured: 23,661, 210 as OT-34/85.

Cost: 188pts (Inexperienced), 235pts (Regular), 282pts (Veteran)
Weapons: 1 turret-mounted heavy anti-tank gun with co-axial MMG and forward-facing hull-mounted MMG
Damage Value: 9+ (Medium Tank)
Options:
- OT-34/85: Replace hull-mounted MMG with flamethrower for +40pts. Flame-throwing vehicles are more likely to be destroyed by damage, as explained on page 52 of the Bolt Action rulebook.

T-35 HEAVY TANK

The T-35 was another enormous (almost ten meters in length) multi-turreted behemoth designed in Russia between the wars. The T-35 had five individual turrets and a crew of 11 men, owing much of its origins to the 'land battleship' concepts of World War I. While it looked impressive in parades, weak armour, poor compartmentalization of the interior and an unreliable transmission made the T-35 little more than a liability in combat. Of the 48 operational in June 1941, only four survived long enough to be withdrawn from service, with most being abandoned due to mechanical breakdown. Due to the relatively thin skin of the T-35, we rate it as only equivalent to a medium tank in damage value. Principal service: 1935–41. Numbers manufactured: 61.

Cost: 216pts (Inexperienced), 270pts (Regular), 324pts (Veteran)
Weapons: 1 turret-mounted light howitzer with co-axial MMG, 1 turret-mounted MMG covering the front and left arcs, 1 turret-mounted MMG covering the rear and right arcs, 1 turret-mounted light anti-tank gun with co-axial MMG covering the front and right arcs, 1 turret-mounted light anti-tank gun with co-axial MMG covering the left and rear arcs
Damage Value: 9+ (Medium Tank)
Special Rules:
- Unreliable: If the T-35 suffers one or more pin markers as a result of an enemy attack, it automatically suffers one further pin marker in addition – such is its extreme operational unreliability.

KV-1 HEAVY TANK

The KV – named after the Defence Commissar Kliment Voroshilov – was a pre-war tank that was thickly armoured all round but also very heavy at 45 tons, making it both unmanoeuvrable and slow. Initially, the 500 KV-1s in service caused the Germans immense problems as the heavy tanks were virtually immune to German anti-tank guns at anything other than point-blank range. This allowed KV-1s to literally overrun German formations in 1941, crushing useless 37mm PaK 36s beneath their broad treads. Although production of the KV-1 continued until 1943, its technical limitations and unreliability were a constant problem, particularly due to a weak transmission system. It was also felt to be undergunned as it carried the same 76.2mm cannon as the smaller and lighter T-34. A flamethrower variant of the KV-1 existed – the KV-8. This took the unusual measure of fitting a 45mm gun with a co-axial ATO-41 flamethrower in the turret, the smaller gun being disguised with a larger fake gun barrel of thin sheet metal to make the KV-8 indistinguishable from normal KVs.

In an effort to improve the mobility of the KV-1 an 'S' (*Skorostnoi* – 'speedy') version was designed in 1942. Armour protection and, therefore, weight was reduced to cut down on strain on the transmission. A new, flatter turret was designed with a commander's cupola with all-round vision blocks – a step forward in Soviet heavy tank design. Existing KV production was turned over to the new S type but the 76.2mm weapon was still felt to be inadequate. In 1943 the appearance of the German Panther spurred renewed work on heavy tanks with larger guns. Once German tanks began to be equipped with guns that could penetrate the KV's heavy armour, its singular advantage over the T-34 was gone. None-the-less, units were still equipped with the KV in the final year of the war, although in diminishing numbers as attrition took its toll upon the survivors. Principal service: 1939–45. Numbers manufactured: KV-1 – 2,874, KV-1S – 1,232, KV-8 – 102.

Cost: 280pts (Inexperienced), 350pts (Regular), 420pts (Veteran)
Weapons: 1 turret-mounted medium anti-tank gun with co-axial MMG, 1 turret-mounted rear-facing MMG, and 1 forward-facing hull-mounted MMG
Damage Value: 10+ (Heavy Tank)
Options:
- KV-1S: Remove the *Armoured all round* bonus and no longer count as *slow* for –70pts.
- KV-8/KV-8S: replace the turret-mounted medium anti-tank gun and co-axial MMG with a light anti-tank gun and co-axial flamethrower for +25pts. Flame-throwing vehicles are more likely to be destroyed by damage, as explained on page 52 of the rulebook.

Special Rules:
- Slow
- Armoured all round: The KV was almost as thickly armoured at the sides and rear as at the front – so no modifiers apply for penetration when shooting at the sides, rear or from above. All shots count the full armour value.

KV-85 AND IS-1 HEAVY TANK

In 1943, the fighting around Kursk–Orel showed the KV-1 had been critically outstripped by German tank development. As a stopgap measure, the KV-85 was produced from the KV-1S hull mated to a turret previously designed for the KV-13 'universal tank' concept with a D5-T 85mm cannon. An entirely new heavy tank design was already on the drawing board for the 'IS' (Iosef Stalin) line and work was begun on this immediately, with the initial production run completed using the same 85mm gun. When it became apparent that T-34s were also being upgunned to 85mm, it was felt that the new heavy tank should pack something bigger, and so the IS-2 was born. While the KV-85 and IS-1 were different tanks, their performance is closely enough matched that they are treated as being the same in Bolt Action terms. Principal service: 1943–45. Numbers manufactured: KV-85 – 130, IS-1 – 100.

Cost: 256pts (Inexperienced), 320pts (Regular), 384pts (Veteran)
Weapons: 1 turret-mounted heavy anti-tank gun with co-axial MMG, 1 turret-mounted rear-facing MMG, and 1 forward-facing hull-mounted MMG
Damage Value: 10+ (Heavy Tank)

IS-2 HEAVY TANK

The Iosef Stalin tank was designed to replace the old KV heavy tank and was a far better-designed machine with thick frontal armour and a huge 122mm gun. Despite this, and the heavy tank classification given to it by the Russians, the IS-2 was only of comparable weight to the German Panther. The IS-2 was intended as a breakthrough tank so it was given a weapon suitable for firing a powerful HE round to clear out enemy strongpoints. After some indecision, the Red Army settled on the

IS-2 heavy tank

same A19 gun-howitzer that was used by the Russian artillery. As an anti-tank weapon this was less potent than its sheer size might suggest. For one thing it was very slow to fire as the shell and charge were separate, and space within the low IS-2 turret was very cramped – two rounds a minute was about all that could be managed. In its role as a tank gun we treat the 122mm gun as a heavy anti-tank gun but with enhanced HE capability. Principal service: 1944–45. Numbers manufactured: 3,854.

THE BRONEKATER – SOVIET RIVERINE CRAFT

The Eastern Front included a surprising amount of coastal and riverine warfare, a fascinating fact commonly obscured by the mammoth scale of the fighting taking place elsewhere. Around the Crimean peninsula and the sea of Azov to the south, and across the Gulf of Finland and the lakes of the Leningrad front in the north, Soviet forces fought from a variety of vessels. Some of the most successful of these were the 'Bronekater'-style of armoured boats frequently referred to as 'tank-ships'. These were armoured, steel-hulled vessels commonly equipped with one or two tank turrets (initially T-28 or BT-7 turrets, but switched to T-34 turrets from 1940), and several minor turrets mounting machine guns. After 1942, some versions of the type 1124 armoured gun boat replaced one of their tank turrets with a Katyusha rocket launcher for direct artillery support. The tank-ships were tough and versatile, designed to be light enough to be lifted out of the water and carried by train to where they were needed. Though the early gun boats displaced thirty tons or less, later types tipped the scales at almost fifty tons. With a laden draft of less than a meter, Bronekaters were used to patrol coastal areas, lakes and rivers, including the Azov, Dnepr, Volga and Danube. They also acted as landing craft for Naval commando forces, and this offers perhaps the most fruitful opportunity to incorporate one into a game of Bolt Action.

In game terms, such an armoured gun boat functions using the tank rules with turrets and weapons appropriate to the model available. While these vessels were less thickly armoured than a conventional tank, their greater size and number of non-essential components made them hard to destroy.

Cost: 240pts (Inexperienced), 300pts (Regular), 360pts (Veteran)
Weapons: 1 turret-mounted medium anti-tank gun with co-axial MMG, 3 turret-mounted MMGs (each in its own turret)
Damage Value: 9+ (Medium Tank)
Transport: Up to 12 men
Options:
- Upgrade 1 turret-mounted MMG to a medium anti-tank gun with co-axial MMG for +65pts
- Replace 1 turret-mounted medium anti-tank gun and co-axial MMG with 1 Katyusha multiple rocket launcher (heavy mortar, multiple launcher) for free
- Upgrade any turret-mounted MMG (except co-axial ones) to twin MMGs (+10pts each), or to a single HMG (+10pts each), or to twin HMGs (+30pts each)

Special Rules:
- Armoured gun boat: No modifiers apply for penetration, all shots count the full armour value. Also, to take into account the Bronekater's size, discard the first damage roll that equal or beats its Damage Value
- Waterborne: May only move in areas of deep or shallow water being treated as a tracked vehicle for speed and turning ability

A Bronekater lurks for unwary prey...

Cost: 256pts (Inexperienced), 320pts (Regular), 384pts (Veteran)

Weapons: 1 turret-mounted heavy anti-tank gun with co-axial MMG, 1 turret-mounted rear-facing MMG, and 1 forward-facing hull-mounted MMG

Damage Value: 10+ (Heavy Tank)

Options:

- May add a pintle-mounted HMG for +25pts

Special Rules:

- HE: Instead of causing D3 HE hits an HE shell causes 2D6 hits
- Slow load: An IS-2 tank cannot be given an order until at least one other unit on the same side has already been given orders (whether successfully or not)

TANK DESTROYERS

The difference between a tank destroyer and self-propelled artillery is somewhat blurred in the Soviet army because most guns were dual purpose – such as the ZiS-3 – and were used as assault guns (short-ranged artillery supporting an infantry attack), self-propelled artillery (for long ranged indirect fire) and anti-tank guns (engaging enemy tanks with armour-piercing shells). The following types are the closest to true tank destroyers – which is to say dedicated to the destruction of enemy armour with powerful anti-tank guns.

ZiS-30

In the desperate days of 1941, Komsomolets tractors were used as improvised tank destroyers, and around a hundred were converted to carry a ZiS-2 57mm anti-tank gun as the short-lived ZiS-30.

The battle for the Ramushevo Corridor, by Peter Dennis © Osprey Publishing Ltd. Taken from Campaign 245: Demyansk 1942–43.

Cost: 96pts (Inexperienced), 120pts (Regular)
Weapons: 1 forward-facing ZiS-2 57mm medium anti-tank gun. 1 forward-facing LMG
Damage Value: 7+ (Armoured Carrier)
Special Rules:
• Open-topped

SU-85

The SU-85 was developed late in 1943 as a stopgap to provide Russian armoured units with a powerful anti-tank gun capable of defeating heavily armoured German tanks such as the Tiger and Panther. It was based on the SU-122 self-propelled gun, itself a development of the T-34 tank with which it shared a basic body. Once the T-34/85 started to become available, production of the SU-85 ceased and it was replaced with the even more powerfully armed SU-100. Principal service: 1943–45. Numbers manufactured: 2,050.

Cost: 176pts (Inexperienced), 220pts (Regular), 264pts (Veteran)
Weapons: 1 casement-mounted forward-facing heavy anti-tank gun
Damage Value: 9+ (Medium Tank)

SU-100

The SU-100 was a up-gunned version of the SU-85 using the 100mm calibre DS10 gun – this weapon had a performance somewhere between the German 88mm as used on the Tiger (Kwk 36) and the superior 88mm gun on the King Tiger (the Kwk 43), but it also had the advantage of a larger shell and hence superior HE capability. It was a formidable weapon and the SU-100 was to continue in Soviet service after the war. Principal service: 1944–45. Numbers manufactured: 1,675.

Cost: 240pts (Inexperienced), 300pts (Regular), 360pts (Veteran)
Weapons: 1 casement-mounted forward-facing super-heavy anti-tank gun
Damage Value: 9+ (Medium Tank)

ISU-122

The ISU-122 was a development of the heavy self-propelled howitzer ISU-152. Both used the same body and chassis, which was also shared with the new IS-2 heavy tank. In practice the ISU-122 proved so popular that more of them were built than the IS-2. The ISU-122 carried the same A-19 gun – itself a combined gun/howitzer, but when mounted onto the ISU-122 it was commonly used in the anti-tank role. We shall treat this weapon as a heavy anti-tank gun but with enhanced HE capability. The large fixed casement of the ISU-122 affords the crew more room to work their gun – so we shall not impose the slow reloading rule as we did for the IS-2. Principal service: 1944–45. Numbers manufactured: 4,075 (mixed with IS-152).

Cost: 240pts (Inexperienced), 300pts (Regular), 360pts (Veteran)
Weapons: 1 hull-mounted forward-facing heavy anti-tank gun
Damage Value: 10+ (Heavy Tank)
Options:
• May add a pintle-mounted HMG for +25pts
Special Rules:
• HE: Instead of causing D3 HE hits an HE shell causes 2D6 hits

SELF-PROPELLED ARTILLERY

The first Russian experiment with self-propelled artillery was the cumbersome KV-2 – an awkward conversion of a KV-1 with a greatly enlarged turret mounting a howitzer for direct fire. However the Russians were greatly impressed by the performance of German STuGs after the invasion and began development of three kinds of self-propelled artillery to support their infantry in April 1942. These were to become the SU-76, SU-122 and SU-152 carrying light, medium and heavy howitzers respectively. All three were based on existing tank chassis, and later they would be joined by the ISU-152 mounting a heavy howitzer based on the IS-2 tank chassis.

TACHANKA

Tachanka were simply horse-drawn carts or wagons with a machine gun mounted on the back. They were a common feature of the Russian Civil War when they were employed with great success to bring fast-moving heavy weapons support to cavalry formations. Purpose-built Tachankas were produced for the Red Army and were deployed with Cossacks and other cavalry. Although by 1941 they were as anachronistic as the cavalry they supported, Tachanka continued to see service until the end of the Great Patriotic War, most commonly on the open steppes of the south. Principal service: 1917–45. Numbers manufactured: Unknown.
Cost: 16pts (Inexperienced), 20pts (Regular), 24pts (Veteran)
Weapons: One rear-facing MMG covering the rear arc
Damage Value: 3+ (Soft-skin)
Special Rules:
• Just a cart: The tachanka moves as a wheeled vehicle. In addition, to represent the vulnerability of the horses, it has been given an unusually low Damage Value, and every time it suffers one or more pin markers as a result of an enemy attack, it automatically suffers one further pin marker in addition

SU-76

The SU-76 was a remarkable weapon that was produced in greater numbers than any other Soviet armoured vehicle aside from the T-34. It was both loved and hated by its crews who referred to it as the *Suka* – 'bitch' – because its thin armour and open top made it vulnerable while its low ground pressure and light weight made it manoeuvrable. The SU-76 was based on the lengthened chassis of the T-70 light tank and featured a dual-purpose 76.2mm ZiS-3 field gun in an open superstructure. It was used as an assault gun, to provide ranged support (at maximum elevation it could fire up to 17km), and also against enemy tanks – a real all-round vehicle. This entry is also suitable for the SU-76P – an improvised conversion of T-26 tanks made by the defenders of Leningrad – and the 'SU-76i' built from Pz IIIs and StuGs captured at Stalingrad. Note that in this case we treat the gun as a light howitzer assuming the vehicle carries only HE shells, and allow an upgrade to alternatively count as an anti-tank gun (the same as the standard Zis-3 divisional gun). Principal service: 1943–45. Numbers manufactured: 12,671.

Cost: 92pts (Inexperienced), 115pts (Regular), 138pts (Veteran)
Weapons: 1 forward-facing light howitzer
Damage Value: 8+ (Light Tank)
Options:

- Versatile: The SU-76 can be equipped with armour piercing ammunition, allowing it to fire its light howitzer as a medium anti-tank gun for +10pts
- SU76i: Remove Open-topped for +5pts

Special Rules:

- Open-topped

SU-122

The SU-122 mounted an adapted M-30 122mm howitzer in an armoured encasement built upon a T-34 chassis. SU-122s were used to equip medium self-propelled artillery regiments and were popular for their powerful punch in infantry support. The M-30 howitzer was poor against tanks, however, even after the advent of shaped charge ammunition. From the beginning of 1944 the SU-122s were gradually phased out by the SU-152 and more heavily armoured ISU-122 and ISU-152. Principal service: 1943–44. Numbers manufactured: 1,148.

Cost: 144pts (Inexperienced), 180pts (Regular), 216pts (Veteran)
Weapons: 1 forward-facing medium howitzer
Damage Value: 9+ (Medium Tank)

SU-76

KV-2

The KV-2 was developed as a close support vehicle to supplement the KV-1 against infantry, guns and bunkers. It mounted a 152mm howitzer in an extremely large box-like turret, bringing the total tank height to almost four meters (12 feet!). Though they were heavily armed and thickly armoured, KV-2s were awkward, cumbersome beasts unable to even rotate their turret when they were not on level ground. They saw service to some effect in the Winter War with Finland, acting as bunker busters against the Mannerheim Line in February 1940. Most of those in service in June 1941 quickly fell victim to mechanical breakdown or the Germans, who put aside captured tanks to use for the planned invasion of Malta. A few KV-2s soldiered on to fight in the battle of Moscow and there are claims some fought at Stalingrad in late 1942. Principal service: 1940–42. Numbers manufactured: Up to 334 by 1941, some sources claim a further 780 were built in 1942 but this seems unlikely and probably refers to the KV-1S.

Cost: 240pts (Inexperienced), 300pts (Regular), 360pts (Veteran)
Weapons: 1 turret-mounted heavy howitzer with co-axial MMG, 1 turret-mounted rear-facing MMG, and 1 forward-facing hull-mounted MMG
Damage Value: 10+ (Heavy Tank)
Options:

- Some KV-2's mounted a flamethrower in the turret. To represent this option, replace the co-axial machinegun with a flamethrower for +45pts. Flame-throwing vehicles are more likely to be destroyed by damage, as explained on page 52 of the rulebook.

Special Rules:

- Slow traverse: A KV-2 cannot be given an order until at least one other unit on the same side has already been given orders (whether successfully or not).
- Slow

SU-152 AND ISU-152

The SU-152 was the most heavily armed of the three self-propelled gun types that entered service in early 1943. It was designed as a mobile heavy howitzer. This was a role hitherto undertaken by the KV-2 tank with a 152mm howitzer in a massive turret. The SU-152 was based on the KV chassis but its forward-facing gun was mounted in an armoured casement. Although designed primarily to smash fortifications and for bombardment of enemy positions, it proved highly effective as a long-range tank killer thanks to the sheer power of its concussive blast. From 1944 onwards the SU-152 was replaced by the ISU-152 which used the chassis of the new heavy tanks – the IS-1 and later IS-2 – but the gun remained the same as did overall performance. Principal service: 1943–45. Numbers manufactured: SU-152 – 704, ISU-152 – 1,885.

Cost: 232pts (Inexperienced), 290pts (Regular), 348pts (Veteran)
Weapons: 1 forward-facing heavy howitzer
Damage Value: 10+ (heavy tank)
Options:
- Can have a pintle-mounted HMG with a 360 degree arc for +25pts

Special Rules:
- Slow load: An SU-152 or ISU-152 cannot be given an order until at least one other unit on the same side has already been given orders (whether successfully or not)
- Big Shell: Because of the sheer size and explosive power of its shell the howitzer has an enhanced Pen value of Pen +5

KATYUSHA

The multiple rocket launcher mounted onto a truck is one of the most distinctively Soviet weapons of the Great Patriotic War. It was a top-secret weapon referred to in official correspondence only by the codename 'Guards Mortars' and operated by specialist NKVD crews until 1942. The noise it made led the German to refer to it as 'Stalin's Organ' but to the Russians themselves it was the Katyusha – *'Little Katie'*. A Katyusha barrage delivered a devastating and highly demoralizing amount of firepower very quickly in a saturation bombardment. It was, however, inaccurate and reloading times were longer than for conventional guns. As a result, Kayushas were generally used to supplement, instead of replace, normal guns, often being employed to open an attack. There were several different types mounting various numbers of rockets – anywhere from 14 to 48 – with those carrying the most rockets requiring considerably longer to reload. All Katyushas were used for long ranged bombardment and most were truck-mounted – their mobility enabling them to disperse quickly after firing to escape the effects of enemy counter-battery fire. Principal service: 1941–45. Numbers manufactured: All types approx 11,000.

Cost: 64pts (Inexperienced), 80pts (Regular), 96pts (Veteran)
Weapons: 1 forward-facing Katyusha multiple rocket launcher (heavy mortar)
Damage Value: 6+ (Soft-skin)
Special Rules:
- Multiple launcher

ANTI-AIRCRAFT VEHICLES

Provision of specialised mobile anti-aircraft vehicles in the Soviet army was poor throughout the war. The only mobile AA vehicles the Red Army had in numbers at the beginning of *Barbarossa* were truck-mounted examples of the Tokarev 4M Model 1931 quadruple Maxim machine gun. While the Red Army remained predominantly on the defensive, it seems that normal tanks and assault guns took precedence over mobile

On to Berlin! Soviet T-34s and their riders

flak and towed AA guns were seen as sufficient. Only once the offensives of 1944 began, an attempt was made to create a 37mm armed anti-aircraft vehicle based on the SU-76, called the ZSU-37, but these did not see service by time of the fall of Berlin. By the late war, the American-built M17 half-track had become available through Lend-Lease, and the Soviet airforce dominated the skies in the east so there was little need to provide ground forces with mobile anti-aircraft cover.

TOKAREV 4M QUAD MAXIM ON GAZ-AAA TRUCK

The quad-mounted anti-aircraft Maxim was developed in 1930 and tested alongside several other quad-, triple- and dual-mount weapons, before being adopted by the Red Army in 1931. The water-cooled Maxims were heavy to start with and mounting four of them on a hefty enough pedestal to absorb their recoil produced a weapon that was only suitable for static emplacement or mounting in the back of a truck. Principal service: 1941–45. Numbers manufactured: Unknown.

Cost: 48pts (Inexperienced), 60pts (Regular), 72pts (Veteran)
Weapons: 4 turret-mounted MMGs

Damage Value: 6+ (Soft-skin)
Special Rules:
- Flak

M17 MGMC ANTI-AIRCRAFT VEHICLE

The M17 MGMC (Multiple Gun Motor Carriage) used the International Harvester-built M5 half-track as the basis for a powerful mobile anti-aircraft gun. It was otherwise comparable to the M16 as used by the Americans and featured a quad .50 cal heavy machine gun. A thousand of these vehicles were sent to Russia via the Lend-Lease program between December 1943 and March 1944. The Russians used their M17s against low flying aircraft and also against ground targets. Principal service: 1943–45. Numbers received: 1,000.

Cost: 100pts (Inexperienced), 125pts (Regular), 150pts (Veteran)
Weapons: 4 turret-mounted HMGs
Damage Value: 7+ (Armoured Car)
Special Rules:
- Open-topped
- Flak

ARMOURED CARS

As with all combatant nations, the Red Army included armoured cars for scouting and sometimes as light support for infantry – notably during street fighting where their small size and manoeuvrability made them especially useful. Large numbers of armoured cars were produced in the 1930s, but few were in use after the first year of war. Most of the Soviet armoured cars were fairly antiquated designs and aside from the creation of the diminutive BA-64, little was done to develop them further, the armoured car's role mostly being taken over by T-60 and T-70 light tanks.

BA-64

The tiny BA-64 'Bobik' ('Bobby') became the standard Russian light armoured car from its first appearance in 1942 and, despite its rather primitive appearance and thin armour, it continued in service until the 1960s. The BA-64 was built on the GAZ-64 Jeep chassis and its angular armour layout was clearly influenced by the German Sd.Kfz 222. Its chief drawback was its sole armament of a single light machine gun in an open turret. The later BA-64B was based on the wider wheel-base GAZ-67 and featured an enclosed turret. On both versions the DT machinegun could fire at a high enough elevation angle to engage enemy aircraft. In 1944 a BA-64DShK version was produced that was armed with a 12.7mm machinegun. Principal service: 1942–45. Numbers manufactured: 9,110 all types.

Cost: 52pts (Inexperienced), 65pts (Regular), 78pts (Veteran)
Weapons: 1 turreted LMG with 360 degree arc
Damage Value: 7+ (Armoured Car)
Options:
- BA-64B: Remove Open-topped for +5pts
- BA-64DShK: Remove Open-topped and upgrade turreted LMG to HMG for +20pts

Special Rules:
- Recce
- Open-topped
- Flak

BA-64 armoured car

BA-20

The BA-20 was an armoured version of the GAZ-M1 civilian car, itself a copy of a Ford design. In June 1941 it was one of the common modern armoured car types available, but its weight and poor off-road ability limited its usefulness as a scout vehicle. BA-20s were phased out of front line service with the arrival of the BA-64 in 1942, although they continued to be used for internal security duties and in the Far East. Principal service: 1936–45. Numbers manufactured: 4,800 all types.

Cost: 52pts (Inexperienced), 65pts (Regular), 78pts (Veteran)
Weapons: 1 turreted LMG with 360 degree arc
Damage Value: 7+ (Armoured Car)
Options:
- Some BA-20s had their machinegun replaced with a flamethrower. To represent this option, replace the turreted machinegun with a flamethrower for +45pts. Flame-throwing vehicles are more likely to be destroyed by damage, as explained on page 52 of the rulebook

Special Rules:
- Recce

BA-10

The BA-10 was a pre-war design that ceased production in 1941, but examples remained in service throughout the war. It was based on the chassis of a GAZ truck and rather unusually carried spare wheels on its side, which also helped the car from grounding when crossing ditches. It packed a 45mm gun in a fully enclosed turret as well as two DT light machine guns. Although classed as a heavy armoured car at 5 tons, its armour was no thicker than 15mm at its greatest, so we rate it with a damage value of 7+ as a 'light' armoured car. Principal service: 1938–45. Numbers manufactured: 3,311 all types.

Cost: 96pts (Inexperienced), 120pts (Regular), 144pts (Veteran)
Weapons: 1 turret-mounted light anti-tank gun with co-axial LMG and 1 forward-facing LMG
Damage Value: 7+ (Armoured Car)
Special Rules:
- Recce

TRANSPORTS AND TOWS

The Russians produced numerous designs of trucks of all sizes from the GAZ staff car and 1½ tonners to larger ZiS 2½ and 3 tonners and as well as heavy cargo trucks such as the YaG 5 and 8 tonners. However, the Western Allies supplied a tremendous number of trucks and other soft-skins under Lend-Lease arrangements, with the Americans alone supplying nearly half a million vehicles of one kind or another. The rugged American trucks were used in all kinds of roles including as tows. British trucks were also supplied in their thousands, including the Bedford 3-tonner, as were Universal or 'Bren' carriers which were used for reconnaissance, as artillery tows, and machine gun carriers. Players wishing to employ these can use the same details as given in the British list (see page 56 for details).

TRUCK

Trucks come in all shapes and sizes and are as likely to be American as Russian – with even a few British examples supplied during the mid-war period. Most general purpose military trucks come in around the 2½–3 ton mark and would mostly be used to transport cargo or as tows for guns. The GAZ 'poltorka' (a licensed Ford 1929 model) was the workhorse of the Soviet army throughout the war.

Cost: 31pts (Inexperienced), 39pts (Regular), 47pts (Veteran)
Weapons: none
Damage Value: 6+ (Soft-skin)
Transport: Up to 12 men
Tow: light howitzer; light or medium anti-tank gun; light or medium anti-aircraft gun
Options:
- May have a pintle-mounted MMG with 360 degree arc of fire for +15pts

GAZ-67 Jeep

HALF-TRACK TRUCK
The Russians produced a number of half-track trucks similar to the German Maultier design. These included the GAZ 1½ ton and ZiS 2½ ton half tracks, which were designed in such a way that the rear track suspension could be lifted and the track removed, allowing the truck to drive on its rear wheels when required.

Cost: 35pts (Inexperienced), 44pts (Regular), 53pts (Veteran)
Weapons: none
Damage Value: 6+ (Soft-skin)
Transport: Up to 12 men
Tow: light howitzer: light or medium anti-tank gun; light or medium anti-aircraft gun
Options:
- May have a forward-facing pintle-mounted MMG covering the front arc for +10pts

GAZ 'JEEP'
The GAZ 67 Command car was inspired by the US-built jeep, which it superficially resembles. The Russians built just under 5,000 by the end of the war – but received more like ten times as many actual Jeeps, so either could be included in a Russian army.
Cost: 17pts (Inexperienced), 21pts (Regular), 25pts (Veteran)
Weapons: none
Damage Value: 6+ (Soft-skin)
Transport: 3 men
Tow: Light anti-tank gun; light anti-aircraft gun
Options:
- May have a pintle-mounted MMG for +15pts, losing all transport capacity
- May upgrade the MMG to a HMG for +10pts

ARTILLERY TRACTORS
The Russians produced a bewildering variety of artillery tractors of all shapes and sizes, including many that resembled fully-tracked trucks with tank underpinnings and truck bodies. Many more were quite literally tractors – adapted from agricultural machines for military use. Tractors were often given armoured bodies, such as the T-26 (based on the chassis of a pre-war light tank).

Cost: 12pts (Inexperienced), 15pts (Regular), 18pts (Veteran)
Weapons: none
Damage Value: 6+ (Soft-skin)
Tow: Any gun or howitzer
Options:
- Field as armoured tractor with damage value of 7+ at +20pts
Special Rules:
- Slow
- Open-topped (if armoured)

T-20 KOMSOMOLETS
The T-20 Komsomolets was an armoured prime mover designed to tow small anti-tank guns. It featured an enclosed crew cabin at the front with a ball-mounted DT light machine gun and exposed benches for the gun crew at the back.

Cost: 48pts (Inexperienced), 60pts (Regular), 72pts (Veteran)
Weapons: 1 forward-facing LMG
Damage Value: 7+ (Armoured Carrier)
Transport: Up to 6 men
Tow: Any anti-tank gun; any anti-aircraft gun; light or medium howitzer
Special Rules:
- Open-topped

T-20 Komsomolets

AEROSAN

The Aerosan was a peculiarly Russian vehicle – a lightly built sled pushed along by a small aeroplane engine. In military hands they were used for scouting over areas of deep snow and ice that were impenetrable to ordinary vehicles. They were also used to support ski-troops, towing supplies or even men. Although restricted to snow and ice, they are interesting vehicles, and the version shown here is the support Aerosan with up to 10mm of armour and a light machine gun.

GAZ-98 Aerosan

Cost: 40pts (Inexperienced), 50pts (Regular), 60pts (Veteran)

Weapons: 1 forward-facing LMG

Damage Value: 7+ (Armoured Carrier)

Transport: Up to 5 Ski Troops (pulling)

Special Rules:

- Snow: The Aerosan can only travel over snow or flat ice – which it treats as normal terrain travelling at the same speed as a wheeled vehicle, but with the same manoeuvrability as a tracked vehicle (1 turn per move)
- Open-topped

LEND-LEASE

The Western Allies supplied prodigious quantities of war materiel to the Soviet Union – over sixteen million tons of it by the end of the Great Patriotic War. This included tanks, guns and aircraft, as well as everything from transport vehicles, canned rations and medical supplies to boots, telephone cable and railway locomotives. The Soviets were dismissive of most of the tanks they were sent, rightly characterising them as poorly armed and/or armoured in comparison to their own tanks. However, given the hideous losses sustained by the Red Army in the fighting, they could ill afford the luxury of not using the fighting vehicles supplied to them. To represent Lend-Lease, Soviet armies themed to follow 1941, can field the following substitute vehicles from Britain and the USA, as described in the appropriate Bolt Action Army Lists:

Tanks/Tank Destroyers
Valentine (substitute for T-60)
M3 Stuart, MK VII Tetrarch
  (substitute for T-70)
M10 Wolverine (substitute for SU-85)
M3 Lee or M4 Sherman
  (substitute for T-34)
Churchill or Matilda
  (substitute for KV-1S)
Armoured cars
M3 Scout Car (substitute for BA-64)

Anti-aircraft vehicles
M17 AA Halftrack (substitute for Tokarev 4M
  Quad Maxim)
Transports and Tows
M5 Halftrack (substitute for Half-track truck)
Bren carrier (substitute for Komsomolets)
Jeep or Seep (substitute for Gaz Jeep)

Soviet Sherman 76

THEATRE SELECTORS

Soviet infantry clearing a pillbox, by Peter Dennis © Osprey Publishing Ltd. Taken from Elite 160:

On an organizational level, the Red Army altered almost beyond recognition between 1941 and 1945.The cumbersome infantry formations and too-widely distributed tank forces of the Red Army contributed to their failure in the summer campaigns of 1941. Heinous losses necessitated that a new, leaner Red Army would be raised almost from scratch. In four years of war, the Soviets learned to mass their forces and firepower along narrow fronts. They learned to keep deep strategic reserves to exploit offensive success or to stabilise collapsing fronts. Most of all they learned how to encircle enemy formations and destroy them. They had learned from the masters of operational command, the Germans, and they had learned their lessons well.

This section contains 18 Theatre Selectors, which we sometimes refer to simply as selectors. Each Theatre Selector draws from the main Army List to describe a force that is broadly appropriate for a particular theatre and period of the Great Patriotic War. Some of the Theatre Selectors overlap in date because, on the 1,200 mile-long Eastern Front, the Red Army was often on the defensive in one area while on the offensive in others. A number of specific selectors are included for each of these phases.

We've placed an emphasis on the infantry-led battles in the East, so many of the Theatre Selectors are set in the northern and central areas of the front, with their denser terrain rather than the open steppes of the south. Equally, by 1943 the Red Army 'settles in' to a cohesive organisation very different from the patchwork of the desperate days of 1941–42. From this point onward, the changing army is mostly defined by the arrival of large numbers of new tanks and heavier guns.

Before playing a game, the players should choose which Theare Selectors they will be using to select their reinforced platoon from. If they so wish, opponents can 'match-up' their army lists to be contemporary with each other, so a Soviet reinforced platoon for Operation Bagration in 1944 would be fighting a German 'Defence of the East' force for 1944. Some Theatre Selectors, particularly the earliest ones when much equipment had been lost, are tailored to a specific time and place in the Red Army's evolution. In general, however, the selectors can be used to represent fighting in the same period on different parts of the front.

Obviously, there is nothing to stop players experimenting and playing against other forces from different periods and theatres. Whilst not historically accurate, players often like to try 'what-if' type games. A particular favourite is pitting Soviet forces against American or British late war formations in a 'Cold War' scenario – a tough proposition for the Western Allies!

ANTI-TANK TEAM THREE-FOR-ONE RULE

Regardless of whether you choose your forces from the generic Platoon Selector or any of the following Theatre Selectors, remember that any mix of up to three anti-tank teams counts as a single pick – meaning the where allowed 0–1 teams you can in fact take 0–3. This extra allowance reflects the high proportion of such teams amongst the Soviet army and is included as a special rule for these teams in the army list. Each unit is still a distinct unit and is represented by a die in the dice cup.

A Soviet force ready for deployment

The famous T-35/85, supported by Red Army infantry

Street-fighting in Kholm, by Peter Dennis © Osprey Publishing Ltd. Taken from Campaign 245: Demyansk 1942–43.

SOME SUGGESTIONS FOR SCENARIOS

The following rules are offered for use in historical games where both players agree. They are intended to reflect the kind of battlefield conditions that prevailed during periods of fighting on the Eastern Front.

THE QUALITY OF QUANTITY

In any game set during the final year of the war from mid-1944 onwards, the Red Army player may substitute the free Inexperienced rifle squad gained through the 'quantity has a quality all of its own' rule with either a free Inexperienced SU-76, medium mortar or ZiS-3 divisional gun.

ANARCHY

The chaos that followed the German invasion resulted in fuel and ammunition shortages that severely hampered the Soviet mechanised forces. In any game set during 1941, tanks, armoured cars, tank destroyers, self-propelled artillery and anti-aircraft vehicles start the game with one pinning marker that may not be removed.

FORESTS AND SWAMPS

Vast areas of the Eastern Front were covered with forests and swamps that made off-road movement difficult even for tanks. All Open Ground is treated as Rough Ground instead.

DEEP SNOW

The Russian winter proved almost as formidable opponent as the Soviet army and the winter of 1941–42 was especially severe. The Russians had learned how to fight in snowbound conditions during the Winter War against the Finns. All open ground counts as Rough Ground for all infantry, artillery, vehicles and non-Soviet tanks due to deep snow.

FROSTBITE

The Germans suffered terribly from the cold conditions of the Russian winter for which they were ill prepared. In a game fought during the winter of 1941–42, each non-Soviet unit must test against leadership at the beginning of the game. If the test is failed, each point by which it is failed indicates the loss of one soldier from the unit in the case of infantry or artillery, or immobilisation in the case of vehicles.

BARBAROSSA!

ATTACK ON THE FORTIFIED REGIONS, JUNE 1941

In accordance with the secret protocols of the non-aggression treaty between Germany and the Soviet Union, in August 1939 large areas of eastern Poland, Romania and the Baltic States had been occupied by the Red Army. Despite weeks of troop build-up, frequent Luftwaffe reconnaissance flights over Soviet territory and warnings from spies and deserters, the German invasion on 22 June 1941 – Operation *Barbarossa* – achieved complete strategic surprise. The Soviet 'fortified regions' along the frontier were pierced at many points by a torrent of fire and steel. To the astonishment of the Germans, many isolated Soviet garrisons resisted to the end even when surrounded and without hope of relief – an ominous foretaste of what was to come.

A Soviet force for the opening of *Barbarossa* must comprise one or more **reinforced platoons** picked from the following Army List. Each reinforced platoon is made up as follows:

FORTIFIED REGION REINFORCED PLATOON

1 Inexperienced Lieutenant – Junior or Senior
2 Inexperienced LMG squads (max 1 LMG per squad) or NKVD squads

Plus:

Headquarters
0–1 Captain
0–1 Commissar
0–1 Medic team
0–1 Forward Artillery Observer

Infantry
0–4 Infantry Squads: Inexperienced LMG squads (max 1 LMG per squad), NKVD squads, Cavalry squads

0–1 MMG team
0–1 HMG team
0–1 Anti-tank team: Anti-tank Rifle team, Ampulomet Anti-tank team, Tank Hunter Anti-tank team (may not have panzerfaust), Dog Mine Anti-tank team
0–1 Mortar team: light, medium or heavy

Artillery
0–1 Gun from:
Anti-tank gun: 45mm Model 1937
Artillery gun: light, medium or heavy
Anti-aircraft gun: 37mm 61-K Model 1939

Armoured Cars
0–1 Armoured car or Recce vehicle from: BA-10, BA-20

Tanks, Tank Destroyers, Self-propelled artillery and Anti-aircraft vehicles
0–1 Vehicle from: T-26 (any variant), BT-5/7, T-37, T-40, T-60, T-28, T-34, T-35, KV-1, KV-8, Tachanka, KV-2, Tokarev 4M Quad Maxim

Transports and Tows
0–1 Transport vehicle per infantry unit in the reinforced platoon from: Truck
0–1 Tow from: Truck, half-track truck, Komsomolets, artillery tractor

SPECIAL RULES
- **Baptism of Fire:** No Soviet forces can be Veteran

Soviet forces prepare to spring their ambush

BATTLE OF KIEV
HITLER'S GREATEST VICTORY, JULY–SEPTEMBER 1941

Germany's Army Group Centre was more heavily reinforced than the invasion groups to the north and south. As a result, a dangerous bulge had developed on the central axis as the Soviet southwestern front held its ground against Army Group South. On the orders of Stalin, more and more reinforcements were poured in to protect Kiev, capital of the Ukraine. Desperate fighting in the battles around Smolensk convinced the German high command that, in spite of its staggering losses, the Red Army was still a danger. In early July, Army Group Centre turned to assist Army Group South and trapped the entire mass of soldiers around Kiev – 43 Divisions – in a huge encirclement. The Red Army suffered 616, 304 dead or captured and 84,240 wounded in the subsequent series of battles. The 43 divisions of the southwestern front virtually ceased to exist in what Hitler called 'the greatest battle in history'.

A Soviet force for the battle of Kiev must comprise one or more **reinforced platoons** picked from the following Army List. Each reinforced platoon is made up as follows:

BATTLE OF KIEV REINFORCED PLATOON

1 Inexperienced Lieutenant – Junior or Senior
2 Rifle squads, Inexperienced LMG squads (max 1 LMG per squad), NKVD squads, Shtrafbat squads or People's Militia squads

Plus:

Headquarters
0–1 Captain or Major
0–1 Commissar
0–1 Medic team
0–1 Forward Artillery Observer

Infantry
0–4 Infantry squads: Rifle squads, Inexperienced LMG squads (max 1 LMG per squad), NKVD squads, Shtrafbat squads, People's Militia squads, Motorcycle squads, Cavalry squads.
0–1 MMG team
0–1 HMG team
0–1 Flamethrower team
0–1 Anti-tank team: Anti-tank Rifle team, Ampulomet Anti-tank team, Tank Hunter Anti-tank team (may not have panzerfaust), Dog Mine Anti-tank team
0–1 Mortar team: light, medium or heavy

Artillery
0–1 Gun from:
Anti-tank gun: 45mm Model 1937
Artillery gun: light, medium or heavy
Anti-aircraft gun: 37mm 61-K Model 1939

Armoured Cars
0–1 Armoured car or Recce vehicle: BA-10, BA-20

Tanks, Tank Destroyers, Self-propelled artillery and Anti-aircraft vehicles
0–1 Vehicle from: T-26 (any variant), BT-5/7, T-37, T-40, T-60, T-28, T-34, T-35, KV-1, KV-8, Tachanka, KV-2, Katyusha, Tokarev 4M Quad Maxim

Transports and Tows
0–1 Transport vehicle per infantry unit in the reinforced platoon from: Truck
0–1 Tow from: Truck, half-track truck, Komsomolets, artillery tractor

SPECIAL RULES
- **Baptism of Fire:** No Soviet forces can be Veteran

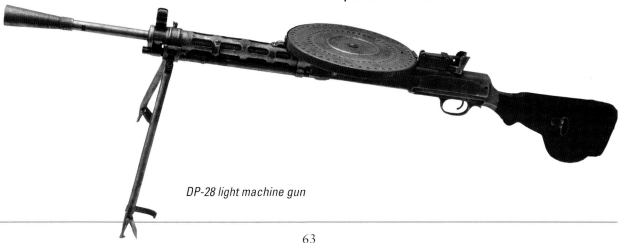

DP-28 light machine gun

ZHUKOV TAKES COMMAND
LENINGRAD APPROACHES, SEPTEMBER–OCTOBER 1941

The German Army Group North had been set Leningrad – the old Tsarist capital of St Petersburg and birthplace of the Revolution – as their primary objective. Fanatical Soviet resistance, thick forests and swamps impeded the Germans' progress but they advanced steadily until they were in position to close a ring of steel around the city in combination with Finnish forces approaching from the North. In September, Marshal of the Soviet Union Giorgi Zhukov was sent to Leningrad as Stavka representative to weld back together its collapsing defences, a task that he performed with astounding alacrity and ruthless efficiency. Leningrad would remain under siege until 1944, but German forces were unable to destroy the city.

A Soviet force for the Leningrad approaches must comprise one or more **reinforced platoons** picked from the following Army List. Each reinforced platoon is made up as follows:

LENINGRAD APPROACHES REINFORCED PLATOON

1 Inexperienced Lieutenant – Junior or Senior
2 Infantry squads: Rifle squads, LMG squads (max 1 LMG per squad), NKVD squads, Shtrafbat squads, Partisan squads, People's Militia squads or Naval Squads

Plus:

Headquarters

0–1 Captain or Major
0–1 Commissar
0–1 Medic team
0–1 Forward Artillery Observer or Forward Air Observer

Infantry

0–4 Infantry squads: Rifle squads, Inexperienced LMG squads (max 1 LMG per squad), NKVD squads, Shtrafbat squads, Partisan squads, People's Militia squads, Naval squads, Motorcycle squads, Cavalry squads
0–1 MMG team
0–1 HMG team
0–1 Sniper team
0–1 Flamethrower team
0–2 Anti-tank team: Anti-tank Rifle team, Ampulomet Anti-tank team, Tank Hunter Anti-tank team (may not have panzerfaust), Dog Mine Anti-tank team.
0–1 Mortar team: light, medium or heavy.

Artillery

0–1 Gun from:
Anti-tank gun: 45mm Model 1937, ZiS-3 Divisional gun, A-19 Field gun
Artillery gun: light, medium or heavy
Anti-aircraft gun: 37mm 61-K Model 1939, 25mm 72-K Model 1940

Armoured Cars

0–1 Armoured car or Recce vehicle: BA-10, BA-20

Tanks, Tank Destroyers, Self-propelled artillery and Anti-aircraft vehicles

0–1 Vehicle from: T-26 (any variant), BT-5/7, T-37, T-40, T-50, T-60, T-28, T-34, KV-1, KV-8, SU-76p, KV-2, Katyusha, Tokarev 4M Quad Maxim

Transports and Tows

0–1 Transport vehicle per infantry unit in the reinforced platoon from: Truck
0–1 Tow from: Truck, half-track truck, Komsomolets, artillery tractor

SPECIAL RULES

• **Baptism of Fire:** No Soviet forces can be Veteran

120mm heavy mortar team

Defenders of Leningrad (L–R): Red Army sergeant, Medical Branch lieutenant, naval infantryman of the Baltic Fleet, by Ronald Volstad © Osprey Publishing Ltd. Taken from Men-at-Arms 216: The Red Army of the Great Patriotic War 1941–45.

SIEGE OF SEVASTOPOL
THE STRUGGLE FOR THE CRIMEA, NOVEMBER 1941–JULY 1942

The great port-city of Sevastopol on the Crimean peninsula was the home base of the Soviet Black Sea fleet and heavily fortified with emplaced artillery, bunkers and minefields as well as the guns of the fleet itself. After their victory at Kiev, the German's Army Group South was ordered to turn its attention to clearing out the Crimea and capturing Sevastopol by Führer Directive 33 on 23 July 1941, but they did not succeed in breaking through along the narrow isthmus connecting Crimea to the Ukraine until October. Soviet forces on the peninsula were strong and they were reinforced both directly and through naval landings made at Kerch on the east of the peninsula in December. The German forces were short of infantry and artillery so they made slow progress against the formidable defences of Sevastopol, only breaching them in June 1942 after months of bombardment performed primarily by the Luftwaffe. The heavy casualties and delays sustained in finally taking the port ensured that German forces in the Crimea were unavailable to support the push for Stalingrad that year.

A Soviet force for the siege of Sevastopol must comprise one or more **reinforced platoons** picked from the following Army List. Each reinforced platoon is made up as follows:

SEVASTOPOL REINFORCED PLATOON

1 (Inexperienced) Lieutenant – Junior or Senior
2 Infantry squads: Rifle squads, LMG squads (max 1 LMG per squad), Veteran squads (may not have panzerfaust and max 1 LMG per squad), People's Militia squads or Naval Squads

Plus:

Headquarters
0–1 Captain or Major
0–1 Commissar
0–1 Medic team
0-2 Forward Artillery Observer or Forward Air Observer

Infantry
0–4 Infantry squads: Rifle squads, LMG squads (max 1 LMG per squad), Veteran squads (may not have panzer faust and max 1 LMG per squad), People's Militia squads, Naval squads
0–1 MMG team
0–1 HMG team
0–1 Flamethrower team
0–2 Anti-tank team: Anti-tank Rifle team, Ampulomet Anti-tank team, Tank Hunter Anti-tank team (may not have panzerfaust), Dog Mine Anti-tank team
0–1 Mortar team: light, medium or heavy

Artillery
0–2 Guns from:
Anti-tank gun: 45mm Model 1937, ZiS-2 Anti-tank gun, ZiS-3 Divisional gun, A-19 Field gun
Artillery gun: light, medium or heavy
Anti-aircraft gun: 37mm 61-K Model 1939, 25mm 72-K Model 1940

Armoured Cars
0–1 Armoured car or Recce vehicle: BA-10, BA-20

Tanks, Tank Destroyers, Self-propelled artillery and Anti-aircraft vehicles
0–1 Vehicle from: T-26 (any variant), BT-5/7, T-37, T-40, T-60, T-28, T-34, KV-1, KV-8, Tachanka, KV-2, Katyusha, Tokarev 4M Quad Maxim

Transports and Tows
0–1 Transport vehicle per infantry unit in the reinforced platoon from: Truck
0–1 Tow from: Truck, half-track truck, Komsomolets, artillery tractor

SPECIAL RULES
• **Baptism of Fire:** No Soviet forces can be Veteran

T-34/76 obr. 1941

OPERATION TYPHOON
DEFENDING THE ROAD TO MOSCOW, OCTOBER–DECEMBER 1941

The original planning for *Barbarossa* had dictated that the Russian capital be captured within the first four months. Bitter Soviet resistance to the north and south plus logistics problems incurred due to the poor roads and worsening weather brought the German advance to a virtual standstill by mid-October. The onset of cold weather froze the ground for long enough for the Germans to renew their offensive against Moscow with Operation *Typhoon*, but by this time Zhukov had been recalled from Leningrad to organise the defences of the capital and fresh Soviet reserves drawn from Siberia were massing. An attempted pincer movement to encircle Moscow was just barely held back as the Germans, who were poorly equipped for the Russian winter, began to suffer severe casualties in both men and machines due to the freezing temperatures.

A Soviet force for the defence of Moscow must comprise one or more **reinforced platoons** picked from the following Army List. Each reinforced platoon is made up as follows:

MOSCOW DEFENDERS REINFORCED PLATOON

1 Lieutenant – Junior or Senior
2 Infantry squads: Rifle squads, LMG squads (max 1 LMG per squad), SMG squads, Guards squads (may not have panzerfaust and max 1 LMG per squad), NKVD squads, Shtrafbat squads, Partisan squads, Cavalry squads, People's Militia squads, Siberian squads, Ski Troops squads or Airborne squads

The Gods of War hammer German positions

Plus:

Headquarters
0–1 Captain or Major
0–1 Commissar
0–1 Medic team
0–1 Forward Artillery Observer or Forward Air Observer

Infantry
0–4 Infantry squads: Rifle squads, LMG squads (max 1 LMG per squad), SMG squads, Guards squads (may not have panzerfaust and max 1 LMG per squad), NKVD squads, Shtrafbat squads, Partisan squads, People's Militia squads, Siberian squads, Ski Troops squads, Airborne Squads, Cavalry squads
0–1 MMG team
0–1 HMG team
0–1 Sniper team
0–1 Flamethrower team
0–2 Anti-tank team: Anti-tank Rifle team, Ampulomet Anti-tank team, Tank Hunter Anti-tank team (may not have panzerfaust), Dog Mine Anti-tank team
0–1 Mortar team: light, medium or heavy

Artillery
0–1 Gun from:
Anti-tank gun: 45mm Model 1937, ZiS-2 anti-tank gun, ZiS-3 Divisional gun, A-19 Field gun
Artillery gun: light, medium or heavy
Anti-aircraft gun: 37mm 61-K Model 1939, 25mm 72-K Model 1940

Armoured Cars
0–1 Armoured car or Recce vehicle: BA-10, BA-20

Tanks, Tank Destroyers, Self-propelled artillery and Anti-aircraft vehicles
0–1 Vehicle from: T-26 (any variant), BT-5/7,T-37, T-40, T-60, T-28, T-34, T-35, KV-1, KV-8, ZiS-30, Tachanka, KV-2, Katyusha, Tokarev 4M Quad Maxim

Transports and Tows
0–1 Transport vehicle **per** infantry unit in the reinforced platoon from: Truck, Aerosan
0–1 Tow from: Truck, half-track truck, Komsomolets, artillery tractor

SPECIAL RULES
- **Battle Hardened:** Only Soviet Headquarters and Infantry units can be Veteran

BLITZFREEZE

THE FASCISTS DRIVEN FROM MOSCOW, DECEMBER 1941–JANUARY 1942

By early December, the exhausted German formations attacking Moscow had been virtually reduced to skeletons by attrition and lack of supply. Some regiments were down to company strength and more than 130,000 cases of frostbite had been reported by German soldiers. As Operation *Typhoon* guttered to a halt, Stavka committed its carefully built-up reserve armies in a general counter-offensive to drive back the Germans. The Germans had been convinced that the Russians had no more reserves to commit and reeled back in confusion before the onslaught. Red Army cavalry, ski-troops and tanks circumvented the road-bound Wehrmacht formations and penetrated deep into the rear. Within weeks the Germans had been thrown back 100–250 kilometres from Moscow and Army Group Centre was teetering on the verge of complete collapse.

A Soviet force for the Moscow counter-offensive must comprise one or more **reinforced platoons** picked from the following Army List. Each reinforced platoon is made up as follows:

MOSCOW COUNTER-OFFENSIVE REINFORCED PLATOON

1 Lieutenant – Junior or Senior
2 Infantry squads: Rifle squads, LMG squads (max 1 LMG per squad), SMG squads, Guards squads (may not have panzerfaust and max 1 LMG per squad), Tank Rider squads, Shtrafbat squads, Partisan squads, Cavalry squads, Siberian squads, Ski Troops squads or Airborne squads

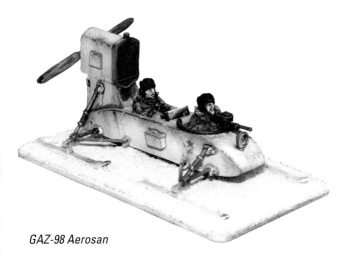

GAZ-98 Aerosan

Plus:

Headquarters
0–1 Captain or Major
0–1 Commissar
0–1 Medic team
0–1 Forward Artillery Observer or Forward Air Observer

Infantry
0–4 Infantry squads: Rifle squads, LMG squads (max 1 LMG per squad), SMG squads, Guards squads (may not have panzerfaust and max 1 LMG per squad), Tank Riders squads, Shtrafbat squads, Partisan squads, Cavalry squads, Siberian squads, Ski Troops squads, Airborne squads
0–1 MMG team
0–1 HMG team
0–1 Sniper team
0–1 Flamethrower team
0–1 Anti-tank team: Anti-tank Rifle team, Ampulomet Anti-tank team, Tank Hunter Anti-tank team (may not have panzerfaust), Dog Mine Anti-tank team
0–1 Mortar team: light, medium or heavy

Artillery
0–1 Gun from:
Anti-tank gun: 45mm Model 1937, ZiS-2 anti-tank gun, ZiS-3 Divisional gun, A-19 Field gun
Artillery gun: light, medium or heavy
Anti-aircraft gun: 37mm 61-K Model 1939

Armoured Cars
0–1 Armoured car or Recce vehicle: BA-10, BA-20

Tanks, Tank Destroyers, Self-propelled artillery and Anti-aircraft vehicles
0–1 Vehicle from: T-26 (any variant), BT-5/7, T-37, T-40, T-60, T-34, KV-1, KV-8, ZiS-30, KV-2, Katyusha, Tokarev 4M Quad Maxim

Transports and Tows
0–1 Aerosan transport vehicle **per** Ski Troops squad in the reinforced platoon
0–1 Tow from: Half-track truck, Komsomolets, artillery tractor

SPECIAL RULES
• **Clapped Out:** Only Soviet Headquarters, Infantry and Artillery units can be Veteran

RZHEV-VYAZMA

OVERPLAYING A GOOD HAND, JANUARY–APRIL 1942

The Moscow counter-offensive drove the fascists back and cut off many of their units, but as the fighting continued, the Red Army found itself unable to crush the Germans. Surrounded Wehrmacht formations grimly hung on in fortified villages and were able to stave off clumsy Soviet frontal attacks while being re-supplied by air drops from the Luftwaffe. Against the advice of his generals, Stalin ordered that the heavily fortified Rzhev–Vyazma salient close to Moscow be liquidated at all costs as part of a further general offensive intended to lift the siege of Leningrad. A series of attacks on the strongly defended salient produced no results and cost the Soviets between 500,000 and 1,000,000 casualties in a battle that became known as 'the Rzhev Meat Grinder'.

A Soviet force for the battle of Rzhev must comprise one or more **reinforced platoons** picked from the following Army List. Each reinforced platoon is made up as follows:

BATTLE OF RZHEV REINFORCED PLATOON

1 Lieutenant – Junior or Senior

2 Infantry squads: Rifle squads, LMG Squads (max 1 LMG per squad), SMG squads, Guards squads (may not have panzerfaust and max 1 LMG per squad), Tank Rider squads, Shtrafbat squads, Partisan squads, Cavalry squads, Siberian squads, Ski Troops squads or Airborne squads

Plus:

Headquarters

0–1 Captain or Major

0–1 Commissar

0–1 Medic team

0–1 Forward Artillery Observer or Forward Air Observer

Infantry

0–4 Infantry squads: Rifle squads, LMG Squads (max 1 LMG per squad), SMG squads, Guards squads (may not have panzerfaust and max 1 LMG per squad), Tank Riders squads, Shtrafbat squads, Partisan squads, Cavalry squads, Siberian squads, Ski Troops squads, Airborne squads

0–1 MMG team

0–1 HMG team

0–1 Sniper team

0–1 Flamethrower team

0–2 Anti-tank team: Anti-tank Rifle team, Ampulomet Anti-tank team, Tank Hunter Anti-tank team (may not have panzerfaust), Dog Mine Anti-tank team

0–1 Mortar team: light, medium or heavy

Artillery

0–1 Gun from:

Anti-tank gun: 45mm Model 1937, M-42 anti-tank gun, ZiS-2 anti-tank gun, ZiS-3 Divisional gun, A-19 Field gun

Artillery gun: light, medium or heavy

Anti-aircraft gun: 37mm 61-K Model 1939

Armoured Cars

0–1 Armoured car or Recce vehicle: BA-10, BA-20, BA-64

Tanks, Tank Destroyers, Self-propelled artillery and Anti-aircraft vehicles

0–1 Vehicle from: T-26 (any variant), BT-5/7, T-37, T-40, T-60, T-34, KV-1, KV-8, KV-2, Katyusha, Tokarev 4M Quad Maxim

Transports and Tows

0–1 Aerosan transport vehicle **per** Ski Troops squad in the reinforced platoon

0–1 Tow from: Half-track truck, Komsomolets, artillery tractor

SPECIAL RULES

- **Clapped Out:** Only Soviet Headquarters, Infantry and Artillery units can be Veteran

Mosin-Nagant carbine with folding bayonet

SECOND BATTLE OF KHARKOV
A NOOSE ALREADY PREPARED, MAY 1942

Despite setbacks at Rzhev, Demyansk and Leningrad, Stalin was convinced that the strategic initiative still rested with the Soviet Union after the winter counter-offensive. He ordered a concentration of forces in the south to retake Kharkov, third-largest city in the Soviet Union and a key industrial centre. A great mass of newly raised rifle divisions and freshly built tanks were thrown into the offensive, but after some initial successes the old Red Army problems of inexperience and poor planning reared their ugly head. Unknown to the Soviets, the Germans had also concentrated forces in the area in preparation for their own summer offensive and were ideally placed to counter-attack. The thrust towards Kharkov was cut off and pounded

Red Army troops descend from their half-track to investigate an abandoned artillery piece

into oblivion by German tanks, planes and artillery, costing the Red Army another 250,000 casualties and the loss of virtually all the tanks and guns committed.

A Soviet force for the second battle of Kharkov must comprise one or more **reinforced platoons** picked from the following Army List. Each reinforced platoon is made up as follows:

SECOND BATTLE OF KHARKOV REINFORCED PLATOON

1 Lieutenant – Junior or Senior
2 Infantry squads: LMG squads (max 1 LMG per squad), SMG squads, Guards squads (may not have panzerfaust and max 1 LMG per squad), Tank Rider squads, Shtrafbat squads, Partisan squads, Cavalry squads, Motorcycle squads

Plus:

Headquarters
0–1 Captain or Major
0–1 Commissar
0–1 Medic team
0–1 Forward Artillery Observer

Infantry
0–4 Infantry squads: Rifle squads, LMG squads (max 1 LMG per squad), SMG squads, Guards squads (may not have panzerfaust and max 1 LMG per squad), Tank Riders squads, Shtrafbat squads, Partisan squads, Cavalry squads, Motorcycle squads
0–1 MMG team
0–1 HMG team
0–1 Sniper team
0–1 Flamethrower team
0–1 Anti-tank team: Anti-tank Rifle team, Ampulomet Anti-tank team, Tank Hunter Anti-tank team (may not have panzerfaust), Dog Mine Anti-tank team
0–1 Mortar team: light, medium or heavy

Artillery
0–1 Gun from:
Anti-tank gun: 45mm Model 1937, M-42 anti-tank gun, ZiS-2 anti-tank gun, ZiS-3 Divisional gun, A-19 Field gun
Artillery gun: light, medium or heavy
Anti-aircraft gun: 37mm 61-K Model 1939

Armoured Cars
0–1 Armoured car or Recce vehicle: BA-10, BA-20, BA-64

Tanks, Tank Destroyers, Self-propelled artillery and Anti-aircraft vehicles (None of these may be Veteran)
0–1 Vehicle from: T-26 (any variant), BT-5/7, T-37, T-40, T-60, T-70, T-34, KV-1, KV-8, Tachanka, Katyusha, Tokarev 4M Quad Maxim

Transports and Tows (None of these may be Veteran)
0–1 Transport vehicle **per** infantry unit in the reinforced platoon from: Truck, half-track truck, Gaz jeep
0–1 Tow from: truck, half-track truck, Komsomolets, artillery tractor

SPECIAL RULES
• **Baptism of Fire:** No Soviet forces can be Veteran

BATTLE OF VORONEZHV

PANZERS BACK ON THE OFFENSIVE, JULY 1942

Flushed with their success at Kharkov, the Germans initiated their summer offensive 'Case Blue' to thrust across southern Russia into the Caucasus and seize the vital oil fields at Baku. Their first objective was capturing the city of Voronezh to gain a bridgehead over the Don river and protect the left flank of their attack. Although both Stalin and the Stavka had by this time embraced the idea of making strategic withdrawals to preserve fighting strength, they were determined to fight for

Soviet forces ambush a German patrol in the foothills of the Caucasus, by Peter Dennis © Osprey Publishing Ltd. Taken from Campaign 184: Stalingrad 1942.

Voronezh. A series of counter-attacks were made against German Panzer forces attempting to capture the city and bloody street fighting there delayed the German advance by several days, which would later prove vital in the battle for Stalingrad.

A Soviet force for the battle of Voronzhev must comprise one or more **reinforced platoons** picked from the following Army List. Each reinforced platoon is made up as follows:

BATTLE OF VORONEZHV REINFORCED PLATOON

1 Lieutenant – Junior or Senior
2 Infantry squads: LMG Squads, SMG squads, Guards squads (may not have panzerfaust), Tank Rider squads, Shtrafbat squads, Cavalry squads, Motorcycle squads

Plus:

Headquarters
0–1 Captain or Major
0–1 Commissar
0–1 Medic team
0–1 Forward Artillery Observer

Infantry
0–4 Infantry squads: Rifle squads, LMG Squads (max 1 LMG per squad), SMG squads, Guards squads (may not have panzerfaust and max 1 LMG per squad), Tank Riders squads, Shtrafbat squads, Cavalry squads, Motorcycle squads
0–1 MMG team
0–1 HMG team
0–1 Sniper team
0–1 Flamethrower team
0–1 Anti-tank team: Anti-tank Rifle team, Ampulomet Anti-tank team, Tank Hunter Anti-tank team (may not have panzerfaust), Dog Mine Anti-tank team
0–1 Mortar team: light, medium or heavy

Artillery
0–1 Gun from:
Anti-tank gun: 45mm Model 1937, M-42 anti-tank gun, ZiS-2 anti-tank gun, ZiS-3 Divisional gun, A-19 Field gun
Artillery gun: light, medium or heavy
Anti-aircraft gun: 37mm 61-K Model 1939

Armoured Cars
0–1 Armoured car or Recce vehicle: BA-10, BA-20, BA-64

Tanks, Tank Destroyers, Self-propelled artillery and Anti-aircraft vehicles
0–1 Vehicle from: T-60, T-70, T-34, OT-34, KV-1, KV-8, Tachanka, Katyusha, Tokarev 4M Quad Maxim

Transports and Tows
0–1 Transport vehicle **per** infantry unit in the reinforced platoon from: Truck, half-track truck, Gaz jeep
0–1 Tow from: Truck, half-track truck, Komsomolets, artillery tractor

SPECIAL RULES
- **Baptism of Fire:** No Soviet forces can be Veteran

BATTLE OF STALINGRAD
STREET-FIGHTING ACADEMY, AUGUST–NOVEMBER 1942

In August, German forces reached the mighty Volga river and entered the major industrial city of Stalingrad, gateway to the east. Stavka had recognised the direction of the fascist attack and ordered Stalingrad prepared for defence, drafting in all available reserves and every citizen between the ages of 15 and 55. Most of the 20-mile long city had been wrecked by Luftwaffe bombing and the defenders dug into the ruins turning every factory, office building and apartment block into a fortress. The Red Army kept their front lines as close as possible to the Germans, frequently interpenetrating the German positions in order to limit their use of artillery and air support. A bloody, gruelling close-quarter battle raged through the city for weeks with ever more German forces being drawn into the maelstrom while the Soviet defenders were sustained by a thin trickle of reinforcements from the east bank of the Volga. Only when the winter weather arrived, and the Soviet counter-offensives began to the north and south, did the Germans in Stalingrad realise they had caught themselves in a trap.

A Soviet force for the battle of Stalingrad must comprise one or more **reinforced platoons** picked from the following Army List. Each reinforced platoon is made up as follows:

PAVLOV'S HOUSE

In mid-September 1942 German troops seized a four-storey apartment house in a dominant position on 9th January square in the middle of Stalingrad. On 22 September, a counter-attack was made by a 30-strong platoon of the 13th Guards Rifle Division led by Junior Sergeant Yakov Pavlov as all of his senior officers and NCOs were dead or wounded at the time. Pavlov and his men recaptured the house after a fierce battle (some accounts say only four of the thirty emerged unwounded). The house was in a key strategic location with a clear line of sight for 1,000 meters to the north, south and west. Sergeant Pavlov was ordered to set up defensive positions to fight off the inevitable German counter-attacks.

Reinforcements were sent to Pavlov over the next few days, including a machine gun platoon commanded by a superior officer, Lt IF Afanasyev, but the location still became known as 'Pavlov's House'. It was defended continuously against multiple daily attacks for 58 days by 25 Red Army soldiers. Pavlov found that by placing his PTRS-41 anti-tank rifle on the roof, the German Panzers could not elevate their guns far enough to hit it and the AT rifle could easily penetrate the thin top armour of the tanks. Machine guns were emplaced in the cellars to fire out at ground level. More machine guns and mortars were positioned in the upper storeys, and barbed wire and minefields in the square below turned the entire area into a death trap. The defenders knocked holes through the basement walls to facilitate easier movement and dug a communication trench with a field telephone line running outside to the Volga for ammunition and reinforcements. Under the call sign 'Lighthouse' the defenders directed Soviet artillery on the east bank of the Volga against concentrations of German tanks and troops as they spotted them.

By mid-November, the defenders of Pavlov's House were having to dash out between German attacks to kick over piles of corpses so that they couldn't be used as cover by the next wave. On German maps, Pavlov's House was marked 'Festung' – fortress – and despite major efforts to eradicate it, the strongpoint remained a thorn in their side throughout the battle. Marshal Chuikov, commander of the defence of Stalingrad, liked to joke that the Germans lost more men trying to take Pavlov's House than they did capturing Paris (not quite true, but almost the case). Yakov Pavlov was decorated for his efforts with the Red Army's highest award, the Hero of the Soviet Union, and went on to survive the war. The four-storey house that bore his name was rebuilt and serves as an apartment building to this day. A memorial there is built of bricks recovered from the east side of the building.

PPSh-41 sub-machine gun – rugged and reliable

BATTLE OF STALINGRAD REINFORCED PLATOON

1 Lieutenant – Junior or Senior

2 Infantry squads: Rifle squads, LMG squads, SMG squads, Guards squads, Veteran squads, NKVD squads, Shtrafbat squads, People's Militia squads, Naval squads, Airborne squads

Plus:

Headquarters

0–1 Captain or Major

0–1 Commissar

0–1 Medic team

0–1 Forward Artillery Observer or Forward Air Observer

Infantry

0–4 Infantry squads: Rifle squads, LMG squads (max 1 LMG per squad), SMG squads, Guards squads (max 1 LMG per squad), Veteran squads (max 1 LMG per squad), NKVD squads, Shtrafbat squads, People's Militia squads, Naval squads, Airborne Squads, Scout squads or a maximum of 1 Assault Engineers squad

0–1 MMG team

0–1 HMG team

0–2 Sniper teams

0–2 Flamethrower teams

0–2 Anti-tank team: Anti-tank Rifle team, Ampulomet Anti-tank team, Tank Hunter Anti-tank team, Dog Mine Anti-tank team

0–1 Mortar team: light, medium or heavy

0–1 Light mortar team

Artillery

0–2 Guns from:

Anti-tank gun: 45mm Model 1937, M-42 anti-tank gun, ZiS-2 anti-tank gun, ZiS-3 Divisional gun, 85mm Model 1939, A-19 Field gun

Artillery gun: light, medium or heavy

Anti-aircraft gun: 37mm 61-K Model 1939, 25mm 72-K Model 1940

Armoured Cars

0–1 Armoured car or Recce vehicle: BA-10, BA-20, BA-64

Tanks, Tank Destroyers, Self-propelled artillery and Anti-aircraft vehicles

0–1 Vehicle from: T-60, T-70, T-34, OT-34, KV-1, KV-1S, KV-8, Tachanka, KV-2, Katyusha, Tokarev 4M Quad Maxim

Transports and Tows

0–1 Transport vehicle **per** infantry unit in the reinforced platoon from: Truck, half-track truck, Gaz jeep

0–1 Tow from: Truck, half-track truck, Komsomolets, artillery tractor

SPECIAL RULES

- **Fanatical Defence:** With their backs to the Volga the defenders of Stalingrad fought with a stubbornness that the Germans found at first nonsensical, then frustrating and finally frightening. An army chosen from this selector can make any infantry units apart from Shtrafbat squads *Fanatics* at an additional cost of +3pts per man

A lend-lease M10 tank destroyer scours the horizon for enemy armour

OPERATION *URANUS*

DEATH ON THE VOLGA, NOVEMBER 1942–FEBRUARY 1943

On 19 November the Red Army unleashed Operation *Uranus*, a twin-pronged attack north and south of Stalingrad with the aim of isolating the German forces in the city. The thinly held flanks of the Nazi positions around Stalingrad quickly caved in beneath the pressure and the arms of the Soviet pincer closed at Kalach on the Don River two days later. The move trapped over a quarter of a million Axis soldiers in and around Stalingrad – 21 field divisions and 100 battalion-sized units. Efforts to break through the Soviet ring were repulsed and attempts to resupply the trapped formations by air proved impossible. Three months later the surviving Germans were forced to surrender, making Stalingrad the first great strategic defeat suffered by the Wehrmacht during the war. There would be many more.

A Soviet force for Operation *Uranus* must comprise one or more **reinforced platoons** picked from the following Army List. Each reinforced platoon is made up as follows:

Naval troops take up a defensive position

OPERATION *URANUS* REINFORCED PLATOON

1 Lieutenant – Junior or Senior

2 Infantry squads: LMG squads, SMG squads, Guards squads, Veteran squads, Tank Rider squads, Shtrafbat squads, Partisan squads, Cavalry squads, Siberian squads, Ski Troops squads, Naval squads or Airborne Squads

Plus:

Headquarters

0–1 Captain or Major

0–1 Medic team

0–1 Forward Artillery Observer or Forward Air Observer

Infantry

0–4 Infantry squads: LMG squads (max 1 LMG per squad), SMG squads, Guards squads(max 1 LMG per squad), Veteran squads(max 1 LMG per squad), Tank Riders squads, Shtrafbat squads, Partisan squads, Cavalry squads, Siberian squads, Ski Troops squads, Naval squads, Airborne Squads, Scout squads or a maximum of 1 Assault Engineers squad

0–1 MMG team

0–1 HMG team

0–1 Sniper team

0–1 Flamethrower team

0–1 Anti-tank team: Anti-tank Rifle team, Ampulomet Anti-tank team, Tank Hunter Anti-tank team, Dog Mine Anti-tank team

0–1 Mortar team: light, medium or heavy

Artillery

0–1 Gun from:

Anti-tank gun: 45mm Model 1937, M-42 anti-tank gun, ZiS-2 anti-tank gun, ZiS-3 Divisional gun, A-19 Field gun

Artillery gun: light, medium or heavy

Anti-aircraft gun: 37mm 61-K Model 1939

Armoured Cars

0–1 Armoured car or Recce vehicle: BA-64

Tanks, Tank Destroyers, Self-propelled artillery and Anti-aircraft vehicles

0–1 Vehicle from: T-60, T-70, T-34, OT-34, KV-1, KV-1S, KV-8, Katyusha, Tokarev 4M Quad Maxim

Transports and Tows

0–1 Transport vehicle **per** infantry unit in the reinforced platoon from: Truck, half-track truck, Gaz jeep

0–1 Aerosan transport vehicle **per** Ski Troops squad in the reinforced platoon

0–1 Tow from: Truck, half-track truck, Komsomolets, artillery tractor

A Tetarch light tank at the vanguard of the Soviet reconnaissance force

OPERATION *STAR*: THIRD BATTLE OF KHARKOV

A FATAL ATTRACTION, FEBRUARY–MARCH 1943

With the Germans in crisis over Stalingrad, Soviet attacks in the south were expanded in scope and aim. Stavka began to think in terms of completely defeating the fascists by liberating the Ukraine in 1943. The Red Army launched Operation *Star* on 2 February – half a million men spearheaded by four tank armies with the objective of recapturing Belgorod, Kursk and Kharkov. Unusually, Hitler granted his commanders freedom of action to deal with the threat and they withdrew, surrendering Kharkov without a fight. On 20 February, the Germans counter-attacked the by-now exhausted and overextended Soviet armies, driving them back out of Kharkov after four days of bitter street fighting. The Germans' other objective, the recapture of Kursk, was prevented by the spring thaw and was destined to be a much tougher battle.

A Soviet force for Operation *Star* must comprise one or more **reinforced platoons** picked from the following Army List. Each reinforced platoon is made up as follows:

OPERATION *STAR* REINFORCED PLATOON

1 Lieutenant – Junior or Senior

2 Infantry squads: LMG squads, SMG squads, Guards squads, Veteran squads, Tank Rider squads, Shtrafbat squads, Partisan squads, Cavalry squads, Siberian squads, Ski Troops squads, Naval squads or Airborne squads

Plus:

Headquarters

0–1 Captain or Major

0–1 Medic team

0–1 Forward Artillery Observer or Forward Air Observer

The Red Army advances relentlessly into the teeth of the Russian winter

Infantry

0–4 Infantry squads: LMG squads (max 1 LMG per squad), SMG
squads, Guards squads (max 1 LMG per squad), Veteran squads
(max 1 LMG per squad), Tank Riders squads, Shtrafbat squads,
Partisan squads, Cavalry squads, Siberian squads, Ski Troops
squads, Naval squads, Airborne Squads, Scout squads or a
maximum of 2 Assault Engineers squads

0–1 MMG team

0–1 HMG team

0–1 Sniper team

0–1 Flamethrower team

0–2 Anti-tank team: Anti-tank Rifle team, Ampulomet Anti-tank team,
Tank Hunter Anti-tank team, Dog Mine Anti-tank team

0–1 Mortar team: light, medium or heavy

Artillery

0–1 Gun from:

Anti-tank gun: M-42 anti-tank gun, ZiS-2 anti-tank gun, ZiS-3
Divisional gun, A-19 Field gun

Artillery gun: light, medium or heavy

Anti-aircraft gun: 37mm 61-K Model 1939

Armoured Cars

0–1 Armoured car or Recce vehicle: BA-64, BA-64B

**Tanks, Tank Destroyers, Self-propelled artillery and
Anti-aircraft vehicles**

0–1 Vehicle from: T-60, T-70, T-34, OT-34, KV-1S,
KV-8, SU-76, SU-76i, SU-122, Katyusha,
Tokarev 4M Quad Maxim

Transports and Tows

0–1 Transport vehicle **per** infantry unit
in the reinforced platoon from:
Truck, half-track truck, Gaz jeep

0–1 Aerosan transport vehicle **per** Ski
Troops squad in the reinforced
platoon

0–1 Tow from: Truck, half-track truck,
Komsomolets, artillery tractor

*Red Army sniper and scout, by Ronald
Volstad © Osprey Publishing Ltd.
Taken from Men-at-Arms 216: The
Red Army of the Great Patriotic War
1941–45.*

BATTLE OF KURSK

DEFENCE IN DEPTH, JULY–AUGUST 1943

After their success at Kharkov, the Germans determined to retain the initiative with a summer offensive aimed against the Soviet salient around Kursk. Two of the most powerful mechanised forces fielded by Germany during the war were concentrated with the objective of cutting off the Soviet armies at Kursk from north and south. The Red Army was to be drained of its strength before it could begin the by now inevitable winter counter-offensive. Stavka correctly predicted the coming offensive and entrenched their forces behind miles of minefields, barbed wire and entrenchments. Vast quantities of Soviet artillery were dug in to form strong points in echeloned defensive belts designed to bleed the Panzer forces white. Behind the defences, thousands of Red Army tanks stood ready to counter-attack once the German assault had exhausted itself. The battle began on 4 July and by 16 July the Germans were retreating to their start lines – the first time the German Blitzkrieg had failed. Successive Red Army attacks liberated Bryansk, Belogrod and Kharkov in July and August. The initiative on the Eastern Front would lie squarely with the Red Army from now on.

A Soviet force for the battle of Kursk must comprise one or more **reinforced platoons** picked from the following Army List. Each reinforced platoon is made up as follows:

BATTLE OF KURSK REINFORCED PLATOON

1 Lieutenant – Junior or Senior
2 Infantry squads: LMG squads, SMG squads, Guards squads, Veteran squads, Tank Rider squads, Shtrafbat squads, Partisan squads, Cavalry squads

Plus:

Headquarters
0–1 Captain or Major
0–1 Medic team
0–1 Forward Artillery Observer or Forward Air Observer

Infantry
0–4 Infantry squads: LMG squads (max 1 LMG per squad), SMG squads, Guards squads (max 1 LMG per squad), Veteran squads (max 1 LMG per squad), Tank Riders squads, Shtrafbat squads, Partisan squads, Cavalry squads, Scout squads or a maximum of 2 Assault Engineers squads
0–1 MMG team
0–1 HMG team
0–2 Sniper team
0–2 Flamethrower team
0–2 Anti-tank team: Anti-tank Rifle team, Tank Hunter Anti-tank team, Dog Mine Anti-tank team
0–2 Mortar team: light, medium or heavy

Artillery
0–2 Gun from:
Anti-tank gun: M-42 anti-tank gun, ZiS-2 anti-tank gun, ZiS-3 Divisional gun, 85mm Model 1939, A-19 Field gun
Artillery gun: light, medium or heavy
Anti-aircraft gun: 37mm 61-K Model 1939

Armoured car
0–1 Armoured car or Recce vehicle: BA-64, BA-64B

Tanks, Tank Destroyers, Self-propelled artillery and Anti-aircraft vehicles
0–1 Vehicle from: T-60, T-70, T-34, OT-34, KV-1S, KV-8, SU-76, SU-76i, SU-122, SU-152, Katyusha, Tokarev 4M Quad Maxim

Transports and Tows
0–1 Transport vehicle **per** infantry unit in the reinforced platoon from: Truck, half-track truck, Gaz jeep
0–1 Tow from: Truck, half-track truck, Komsomolets, artillery tractor

T-34/76 obr. 1943 and tank riders

*Heroes of Kursk (L–R): Red Army lieutenant, sniper, tank crewman, by Ronald Volstad © Osprey Publishing Ltd.
Taken from Men-at-Arms 216:* The Red Army of the Great Patriotic War 1941–45.

LENINGRAD-NOVGOROD OFFENSIVE

THE END OF 900 DAYS OF TERROR, JANUARY 1944

In January 1943, the Soviet Operation *Iskra* ('*Spark*') had opened a narrow land corridor to Leningrad, but the city remained besieged through the rest of the year. In January 1944, once the ice on Lake Ladoga had thickened sufficiently to move tanks and artillery to the front, the Soviets went on the offensive in an effort to break the siege altogether. Their opponents, Army Group North, had already been weakened by the reassignment of some of their most experienced divisions to attempt to stem Red Army breakthroughs far to the south. The first few days of the Soviet operation were hampered by thick fog, but the Red Army pushed steadily forward. Thanks to the dense, heavily fortified terrain, the Germans were able to retreat in an orderly fashion to the 'Panther Line' near the river Narva with the Red Army snapping at their heels every step of the way. The siege of Leningrad was finally lifted after 900 days, an event celebrated with a 324 gun salute (including Katyushas!) on 27 January 1944.

A Soviet force for the Leningrad–Novgorod offensive must comprise one or more **reinforced platoons** picked from the following Army List. Each reinforced platoon is made up as follows:

SU-76 with infantry support

T-34/76 obr.1942 medium tank

LENINGRAD–NOVGOROD REINFORCED PLATOON

1 Lieutenant – Junior or Senior
2 Infantry squads: LMG squads, SMG squads, Guards squads, Veteran squads, Tank Rider squads, Shtrafbat squads, Partisan squads, Cavalry squads, Ski Troops squads

Plus:

Headquarters
0–1 Captain or Major
0–1 Medic team
0–1 Forward Artillery Observer or Forward Air Observer

Infantry
0–4 Infantry squads: LMG squads (max 1 LMG per squad), SMG squads, Guards squads (max 1 LMG per squad), Veteran squads (max 1 LMG per squad), Tank Riders squads, Shtrafbat squads, Partisan squads, Cavalry squads, Scout squads or a maximum of 2 Assault Engineers squads, Ski Troops squads
0–1 MMG team
0–1 HMG team
0–1 Sniper team
0–1 Flamethrower team
0–1 Anti-tank team: Anti-tank Rifle team, Tank Hunter Anti-tank team
0–1 Mortar team: light, medium or heavy

Artillery
0–1 Gun from:
Anti-tank gun: M-42 anti-tank gun, ZiS-2 anti-tank gun, ZiS-3 Divisional gun, 85mm Model 1939, A-19 Field gun
Artillery gun: light, medium or heavy
Anti-aircraft gun: 37mm 61-K Model 1939

Armoured Cars
0–1 Armoured car or Recce vehicle: BA-64, BA-64B

Tanks, Tank Destroyers, Self-propelled artillery and Anti-aircraft vehicles
0–1 Vehicle from: T-37, T-40, T-50, T-60, T-70, T-34, OT-34, KV-1S, KV-8, KV-85/IS-1, SU-76, SU-85, SU-122, SU-152, Tachanka, Katyusha, Tokarev 4M Quad Maxim

Transports and Tows
0–1 Transport vehicle **per** infantry unit in the reinforced platoon from: Truck, half-track truck, Gaz jeep, Aerosan
0–1 Tow from: Truck, half-track truck, Komsomolets, artillery tractor

OPERATION *BAGRATION*

THE DESTRUCTION OF ARMY GROUP CENTRE, JUNE–AUGUST 1944

As predicted, the Red Army winter offensive was devastating and for the rest of the year the Germans were in almost constant retreat. Smolensk and Kiev were liberated by the advancing Soviet armies and the Ukraine virtually cleared by the end of 1943. To the north, the siege of Leningrad was finally lifted early in 1944. By the summer of 1944, the Red Army had reached the borders of Belorussia and eastern Poland where the German defences were firmly anchored by fortifications and minefields across much of the front. The Red Army was a very different entity to that of 1941–42. By now large Soviet mechanised formations and tank armies were capable of the kind of mobile warfare and deep exploitation the Wehrmacht had used to subjugate all of Western Europe. New heavy tanks and tank destroyers had been created to face the Germans' Tiger and Panther tanks, denying them even that technical edge against the overwhelming hordes they faced.

A Soviet force for operation Bagration must comprise one or more **reinforced platoons** picked from the following Army List. Each reinforced platoon is made up as follows:

OPERATION *BAGRATION* REINFORCED PLATOON

1 Lieutenant – Junior or Senior
2 Infantry squads: LMG squads, SMG squads, Guards squads, Veteran squads, Tank Rider squads, Shtrafbat squads, Partisan squads, Cavalry squads

Plus:

Headquarters

0–1 Captain or Major
0–1 Medic team
0–2 Forward Artillery Observer or Forward Air Observer

Infantry

0–4 Infantry squads: LMG squads (max 1 LMG per squad), SMG squads, Guards squads (max 1 LMG per squad), Veteran squads (max 1 LMG per squad), Tank Riders squads, Shtrafbat squads, Partisan squads, Cavalry squads, Scout squads or Assault Engineers squads
0–1 MMG team
0–1 HMG team
0–1 Sniper team
0–1 Flamethrower team
0–1 Anti-tank team: Anti-tank Rifle team, Tank Hunter Anti-tank team.
0–1 Mortar team: light, medium or heavy.

Artillery

0–2 Gun from:
Anti-tank gun: 45mm Model 1937, M-42 anti-tank gun, ZiS-2 anti-tank gun, ZiS-3 Divisional gun, A-19 Field gun, BS-3 anti-tank gun
Artillery gun: light, medium or heavy
Anti-aircraft gun: 37mm 61-K Model 1939

Armoured Cars

0–1 Armoured car or Recce vehicle: BA-64, BA-64B, BA-64DShK

Tanks, Tank Destroyers, Self-propelled artillery and Anti-aircraft vehicles

0–1 Vehicle from: T-60, T-70, T-34, OT-34, T-34/85, OT-34/85, KV-85/IS-1, IS-2, SU-85, ISU-122, Tachanka, SU-76, SU-122, SU-152, Katyusha, Tokarev 4M Quad Maxim

Transports and Tows

0–1 Transport vehicle **per** infantry unit in the reinforced platoon from: Truck, half-track truck, Gaz jeep
0–1 Tow from: Truck, half-track truck, Komsomolets, artillery tractor

Tokarev SVT-40 semi-automatic rifle

VISTULA-ODER OFFENSIVE

INTO THE REICH, JANUARY-FEBRUARY 1945

The success of Operation *Bagration* carried the Red Army all the way across eastern Poland to the Vistula River and the capital, Warsaw. With shocking ruthlessness, the Soviets remained inactive through the autumn while the Poles attempted an uprising in Warsaw and the Germans punished them horrifically for their courage. The Red Army advance was renewed in January 1945 as the Soviet tanks broke out of their bridgeheads on the Vistula and set their sights on the River Oder – a little more than forty miles from Berlin. By the Vistula–Oder offensive, the Soviets outnumbered the Germans five to one in men, guns, tanks and aircraft. Veteran Wehrmacht survivors were still exacting a dreadful toll on the Red Army, but for the disintegrating Third Reich it was now only a matter of time before the final blow fell.

A Soviet force for the Vistula–Oder offensive must comprise one or more **reinforced platoons** picked from the following Army List. Each reinforced platoon is made up as follows:

VISTULA-ODER OFFENSIVE REINFORCED PLATOON

1 Lieutenant – Junior or Senior
2 Infantry squads: LMG squads, SMG squads, Guards squads, Veteran squads, Tank Rider squads, Shtrafbat squads, Cavalry squads

Plus:

Headquarters
0–1 Captain or Major
0–1 Medic team
0–2 Forward Artillery Observer or Forward Air Observer

Infantry
0–4 Infantry squads: LMG squads (max 1 LMG per squad), SMG squads, Guards squads (max 1 LMG per squad), Veteran squads (max 1 LMG per squad), Tank Riders squads, Shtrafbat squads, Cavalry squads, Scout squads or Assault Engineers squads
0–1 MMG team
0–1 HMG team
0–1 Sniper team
0–1 Flamethrower team
0–1 Anti-tank team: Anti-tank Rifle team, Tank Hunter Anti-tank team
0–2 Mortar teams: light, medium or heavy

Artillery
0–2 Gun from:
Anti-tank gun: 45mm Model 1937, M-42 anti-tank gun, ZiS-2 anti-tank gun, ZiS-3 Divisional gun, A-19 Field gun, BS-3 anti-tank gun
Artillery gun: light, medium or heavy
Anti-aircraft gun: 37mm 61-K Model 1939

Armoured Cars
0–1 Armoured car or Recce vehicle: BA-64, BA-64B, BA-64DShK

Tanks, Tank Destroyers, Self-propelled artillery and Anti-aircraft vehicles
0–1 Vehicle from: T-60, T-70, T-34, OT-34, T-34/85, OT-34/85, IS-2, SU-85, ISU-122, Tachanka, SU-76, SU-100, SU-152, Katyusha, Tokarev 4M Quad Maxim

Transports and Tows
0–1 Transport vehicle **per** infantry unit in the reinforced platoon from: Truck, half-track truck, Gaz jeep
0–1 Tow from: Truck, half-track truck, Komsomolets, artillery tractor

Soviet Engineers redeploy

SEELOW HEIGHTS

THE GATES OF BERLIN, APRIL 1945

The extended Soviet spearheads turned aside in March to clear their flanks of German forces in Pomerania and East Prussia, before making the final drive on Berlin in April. The last major defensive line before reaching the capital was the Seelow Heights, a low range of hills overlooking the river Oder where it was crossed by the east–west Berlin autobahn. While Soviet armies attacked to the north and south, Marshal Zhukov was given the task of breaching the last, and toughest, defences of World War II. Even when outnumbered ten to one, German tactical flair allowed them to once again delay the inevitable and inflict heavy casualties on the Red Army, but after four days of bloody fighting, the way to Berlin was open.

A Soviet force for the Seelow Heights must comprise one or more **reinforced platoons** picked from the following Army List. Each reinforced platoon is made up as follows:

A T-34/76 hunts Fascist prey...

SEELOW HEIGHTS REINFORCED PLATOON

1 Lieutenant – Junior or Senior
2 Infantry squads: LMG squads, SMG squads, Guards squads, Veteran squads, Tank Rider squads, Shtrafbat squads, Assault Engineers squads

Plus:

Headquarters

0–1 Captain or Major
0–1 Medic team
0–2 Forward Artillery Observer or Forward Air Observer

Infantry

0–4 Infantry squads: LMG squads (max 1 LMG per squad), SMG squads, Guards squads (max 1 LMG per squad), Veteran squads (max 1 LMG per squad), Tank Riders squads, Shtrafbat squads, Scout squads or Assault Engineers squads
0–1 MMG team
0–1 HMG team
0–1 Sniper team
0–1 Flamethrower team
0–1 Anti-tank team: Anti-tank Rifle team, Tank Hunter Anti-tank team
0–2 Mortar teams: light, medium or heavy

Artillery

0-2 Gun from:
Anti-tank gun: 45mm Model 1937, M-42 anti-tank gun, ZiS-2 anti-tank gun, ZiS-3 Divisional gun, A-19 Field gun, BS-3 anti-tank gun
Artillery gun: light, medium or heavy
Anti-aircraft gun: 37mm 61-K Model 1939

Armoured Cars

0–1 Armoured car or Recce vehicle: BA-64, BA-64B, BA-64DShK

Tanks, Tank Destroyers, Self-propelled artillery and Anti-aircraft vehicles

0–2 Vehicle from: T-60, T-70, T-34, OT-34, T-34/85, OT-34/85, IS-2, SU-85, ISU-122, SU-76, SU-100, SU-152, Katyusha, Tokarev 4M Quad Maxim

Transports and Tows

0–1 Transport vehicle **per** infantry unit in the reinforced platoon from: Truck, half-track truck, Gaz jeep
0–1 Tow from: Truck, half-track truck, Komsomolets, artillery tractor

BERLIN

DEATH OF THE THIRD REICH, APRIL–MAY 1945

Soviet forces began their bombardment of Berlin on 20 April 1945. For the final act, Stavka encircled the German capital over the next three days with 2.5 million men, 6,250 tanks, and almost 45,000 artillery pieces. The shattered divisions facing them were a mixture of Volkssturm militia, Wehrmacht troops, Hitler Youth and SS units clinging to concentric rings of defences in the bombed-out ruins of Berlin. Fierce street battles raged for a week as the Soviet forces pushed into the heart of Berlin, blasting their way forward with heavy tank support in the face of panzerfausts and fanatical resistance.

On 30 April, as Red Army soldiers fought to capture the Reichstag, Adolf Hitler committed suicide inside his Fuhrerbunker. Two days later, Berlin was surrendered to Marshal Chuikov, the redoubtable defender of Stalingrad. In Europe, World War II was all but over.

A Soviet force for the Seelow Heights must comprise one or more **reinforced platoons** picked from the following Army List. Each reinforced platoon is made up as follows:

BERLIN REINFORCED PLATOON

1 Lieutenant – Junior or Senior
2 Infantry squads: LMG squads, SMG squads, Guards squads, Veteran squads, Tank Rider squads, Shtrafbat squads, Assault Engineers squads

Plus:

Headquarters

0–1 Captain or Major
0–1 Medic team
0–1 Forward Artillery Observer or Forward Air Observer

Infantry

0–4 Infantry squads: LMG squads (max 1 LMG per squad), SMG squads, Guards squads (max 1 LMG per squad), Veteran squads (max 1 LMG per squad), Tank Riders squads, Shtrafbat squads, Scout squads or Assault Engineers squads
0–1 MMG team
0–1 HMG team
0–1 Sniper team
0–1 Flamethrower team
0–1 Anti-tank team: Anti-tank Rifle team, Tank Hunter Anti-tank team
0–1 Mortar team: light, medium or heavy

Artillery

0–1 Gun from:
Anti-tank gun: 45mm Model 1937, M-42 anti-tank gun, ZiS-2 anti-tank gun, ZiS-3 Divisional gun, A-19 Field gun, BS-3 anti-tank gun
Artillery gun: light, medium or heavy
Anti-aircraft gun: 37mm 61-K Model 1939

Armoured Cars

0–1 Armoured car or Recce vehicle: BA-64, BA-64B, BA-64DShK

Tanks, Tank Destroyers, Self-propelled artillery and Anti-aircraft vehicles

0–2 Vehicle from: T-60, T-70, T-34, OT-34, T-34/85, OT-34/85, IS-2, SU-85, ISU-122, SU-76, SU-100, SU-152, Katyusha, Tokarev 4M Quad Maxim

Transports and Tows

0–1 Transport vehicle **per** infantry unit in the reinforced platoon from: Truck, half-track truck, Gaz jeep
0–1 Tow from: Truck, half-track truck, Komsomolets, artillery tractor

Soviet Sherman 75

Urban warfare in Berlin, by Peter Dennis © Osprey Publishing Ltd. Taken from Campaign 159: Berlin 1945.